THE REAL ITALIANS

THE REAL ITALIANS

A Study in European Psychology

By CARLO SFORZA

COLUMBIA UNIVERSITY PRESS

NEW YORK · 1942

Copyright 1942

COLUMBIA UNIVERSITY PRESS, NEW YORK

Foreign agents: Oxford University Press, Humphrey Milford, Amen House, London, E.C. 4, England, and B. I. Building, Nicol Road, Bombay, India

MANUFACTURED IN THE UNITED STATES OF AMERICA

———

Translated from *Les Italiens tels qu'ils sont*, Montreal, 1941, with the addition of Chapters XII and XVI.

To the Italians and sons of Italians in Canada and the two Americas I dedicate these pages, dictated by an unshaken faith in our future: that future when—once again a free people—we shall all have realized that the integrity of our national life and the future of our country hang on the coming of that free and federated Europe of which Mazzini was the first prophet.

PREFACE

IN SPITE OF the striking appearances of political changes, men are still more affected by the thinking of their ancestors than by ideas special to their generation. To understand a people we must know its origins and history. This is what I have tried to do in the first part of this book. It is not my fault if this takes us back to pre-Roman times.

The surprising thing may seem, not what is in the book, but what has been left out of it. Those unfamiliar with Italy naturally expect much about fascism. But from the first day of fascism I declared that its regime might involve Italy in political adventures fatal to the very life of my country. I repeated this in spite of Mussolini's bids for my collaboration. The facts have borne me out. The fascist wars with Ethiopia, Spain, France, England, and Greece have been squarely against the essential interests of Italy.

Fascism is empty show despite its boastings, as all Italians know. Why talk as if it were a living force? In the long history of Italy only those movements have survived which have had some moral truth and aspired toward some ideal. Even though we admit that at the beginning its more naïve adherents were sincere, the fascist movement has never met these requirements.

There are other gaps in this book for which I would apologize if I were an expert in mass psychology or a man of letters. I pretend to be neither. My constant rule has been to put into this book only what "I have learned by unceasing study and long experience in the way the world works."

These words are Machiavelli's, from the Preface of his immortal *Discourses*. Even the great Florentine, cool and detached as he was, sometimes let theory carry him away. In my case not pride but modesty makes me repeat his words.

One thing more—knowing that Italians, great and small, are both simple and complex, I have written in the hope of making certain writers about Italy hesitate over ready-made axioms and truisms concerning Italians, about which those who know can only smile. Is this too much to hope?

Of one thing I am sure: much as I love my country, I have refrained from patriotic and pseudo-patriotic dithyramb. Perhaps this is because I love my country even more in its trials than in its glories. But if sometimes my filial tenderness shows through, I can only repeat what Goethe's Neapolitan coachman said to him as they drove about Naples:

"What else would you have? This is my own country."

SFORZA

New York
1941

CONTENTS

I. The Historical Origins of the Italians   1

II. Why Their History Has Made the Italians Discontented Internationalists   8

III. And Why This Discontent Has Produced the Principal Defect of a Part of the Italian Middle Class: Fustian   15

IV. The Italians and Their Literature   22

V. The Italians and Their Dialects   35

VI. The Italians and Their Roots in the Soil   41

VII. Italians and the Family Bond   53

VIII. The Italians and Their Religion   58

IX. Italians of the North and Italians of the South   69

X. Italy and Foreign Visitors and Writers   76

XI.   *The Italians and Their French Neighbors*   84

XII.   *The Italians and Their Swiss Neighbors*   96

XIII. *The Italians and Their German Neighbors*   101

XIV.   *The Italians and Their Yugoslav Neighbors* 106

XV.   *The Italians and Their English Neighbors*   111

XVI.   *The Italians and America*   116

XVII. *Anti-Italian Legends: Italian Skepticism*   132

XVIII. *Anti-Italian Realities: Fascism*   137

XIX.   *The Italians and the Future of Europe*   141

Recent Books on Italian Problems   155

CHAPTER I

The Historical Origins of the Italians

FOR ALL PRACTICAL PURPOSES the history of the essential characteristics of today's Italians goes back four or five centuries before Christ, to the Etruscans between the Arno and the Tiber and the Greek colonists who had settled in the South. The latter established in the lower peninsula and Sicily a typically Greek civilization, in which the city was the one base of the whole political and social system. Similarly, pre-Roman Etruria was only a confederation of twelve politically independent cities, closely united by religious bonds. The city remained the base of Italian social life after the Romans conquered the whole peninsula.

No other nation in the world has shown such need of attaching its traditions, fables, and folk poetry to its cities. In the Middle Ages, while the French sang of Roland, Italian rhymes taught that Rome was descended from Alba Longa, as Alba Longa descended from Lavinium, and Lavinium from Troy. From this comes the long-lived reputation of Virgil among the common folk of Italy; he made the history of their country an evolution of city from city—the only form of history which could please Italians.

Even today the names of the regions of Italy—like Piedmont, Lombardy, and Liguria—mean little to ordinary people. The villager from Liguria, the region which sweeps down the coast from the French border to Genoa

and southward to the mouth of the Magra, would not call
himself "Ligurian" but "Genoese," or at least he would
say that he was "from the *Genovesato*." It has always been
like this in Italy. In Gaul, more often than not, the name
of the surrounding region became the name of the city:
Lutetia, the city of the Parisii, is now Paris; Avaricum,
capital of the Biturgi, became Bourges; the process was
the same with Amiens, Rheims, Rennes, and numerous
other cities.

The peasant's way of identifying himself with the neighboring city constitutes one of the most permanent elements
of the Italian social structure. In no other country is normal, healthy, fruitful patriotism (not racism or nationalism) so bound up primarily with the city, the *municipio*.
De Sanctis, who wrote the best of all the numerous histories of our literature, said to the Neapolitans in 1874:
"Italy, gentlemen, is no abstraction; she is the home, the
family, and the province, and the region. They are the best
Italians who feel themselves bound to these things. . . .
I say to you; if you want to be good Italians, start by being
good Neapolitans. . . . Woe to him who sees in Italy
only an academic word, a schoolbook concept." Thus, fifty
years before fascism De Sanctis condemned one of the
most unnatural of fascist enterprises, the struggle against
the ancient traditions of local patriotism. Right here fascism revealed at once how alien it is to the Italian character.

The ancient bond between generations of Italians is the
city, the *municipio*. Its history reaches back to pre-Roman
times. Still active minor jealousies between Milan and
Pavia, Crema and Cremona, as well as the differences in

the local speech, are traditions which pre-date the Empire.

When Rome came to dominate all Italy, almost every *municipium* from the Alps to Sicily had to give up a parcel of its land to a Latin colony, which imposed its ways, manners, and language, so that the majority of natives came to speak Latin, although with a local accent. Today the traveler who goes from Rome through Florence into the Lunigiana to Piacenza and on to Milan finds in the sharp demarcation of the dialects the line of separation between different *gentes* of ancient times. Beyond the Alps, on the German side, this is not true. There the frequent migrations and the absence of definite frontiers never permitted the formation of such distinct local characteristics.

Under republican Rome, Italy was never really more than an immense federation of self-governing cities—having a system somewhat like that of the British people now that they have abandoned the proud "empire" for the democratic "commonwealth." It was the Roman Empire, beginning with Hadrian, which first showed signs of decadence. Until then the cities and the colonies had been governed by the moneyed, active bourgeoisie which produced the Flavians. The duumvirs, chosen among notable taxpayers, carried on the administration from the Tribunal. In Hadrian's reign the offices of the imperial administration took over local affairs one by one. Under Diocletian what we would call the "integral state" was completely established. Even the *defensor civitatis* was no longer anything more than a functionary who was expected, naïvely or hypocritically, to denounce the errors of his superiors. The old *curiae*, once freely elected by the citizens, became lifeless corporations fettered by innumerable bonds. Soon military pride and distrust of the citizenry left nothing but prefectures entrusted to *comites* sent from the capital. Under the Eastern Empire these *comites*, still further corrupted, were called "duces," whence the name "doge," for centuries the title of the chiefs of the aristocratic republics of Venice and Genoa.

Under Diocletian barbarism had already invaded Italy, as the result of third-century military anarchy rather than of the descent of a few famished tribes from Germany. The later reputation of these "irresistible invaders" is the product of German vanity and the Italian desire to attribute misfortune to an exterior cause.

This ancient and empty German boast has become an official Nazi dogma. The schools of the *Reich* are obliged to teach the rising generations the "capital role played by the Germanic migrations in the spread of medieval civilization through northern Italy, France, and England." What will young Germans think if they ever leave Nazi schools and learn that the Goths dominated Italy only sixty years, that in Spain they were beaten by some Semites called Arabs and in a single day lost all they had, that though they had been invited by part of the population, the Longobards never succeeded in occupying the coast or dared attack either the powerful defenses of Venice or the old ramparts of Rome, and that their domination ended in cowardly confusion?

But for the degeneration brought about by the military anarchy and the bureaucratic despotism of the Empire, the German clans would never have got into Italy. The resistance of the Italian cities would have been enough. But the Empire had sapped away their life.

On the eve of catastrophe, under Constantine, it looked for a moment as if barbarism could be quelled. The cities appeared ready for a rebirth of vitality. A certain disguised autonomy had been established under the leadership of the bishops, all of whom were elected by the citizens, since the election through acclamation of a bishop was generally the result of a genuine movement among the people. But it was too late. The crushing taxes and the habit of sending military chiefs to govern cities where they were strangers had drawn off the last drop of life from the Italian cities. They had become cities of death—dead as the great capitals of Turkey and Persia, for example, appeared to our fathers in the nineteenth century.

Istanbul and Teheran were no less rich and no less beautiful than medieval Naples or Milan; a Turkish art existed still, and so did a Persian. But since they were cities without municipal liberty and without autonomous life, they were therefore servile cities. If Byzantium, before it became "Stambul," did manage to preserve a bit of life, it was because the municipal tradition had not been destroyed by the government of the *Basileus* as it had been destroyed in Italy by the Caesars. The *Demes*—divisions comparable to the *contrade* of Siena—remained strongholds of municipal life. So did the corporations, as the tenth-century *Book of the Prefect* shows them in their relative freedom. The *Demes* and the free corporations hold the key to the real life, the sudden bursts of resistance, and the revolutions of Byzantium.

But Byzantium was a unique exception. The other metropolitan cities of the East, despite their occasional magnificence, were inert. They had discipline, but not one atom of that quivering energy which animated the anarchical Athens of Aristophanes even at its worst.

On the other hand, the German dominations of Italy, except that of the Longobards, were so short and left so little imprint because they did not reckon with the strength of Italian municipal life. A sort of "inferiority complex" kept the Germans away from the cities, where they felt on one hand the persisting splendor of the imperial regime and on the other the mysterious germination of the new Italian life to come. This naïve German ignorance of the cities made them apply their crude rural conceptions to a country in which the city was all-important. This is why they left no more trace than the German armies have left in Poland, France, the Netherlands, and Czechoslovakia.

Alive, these Italian cities? Alive and more—each of them is a world in itself. And foreigners who, like Edgar Quinet, have wept over the persistent hatreds and rancors the cities bear each other have never seen that in reality these passions are of the type which astonish nobody when they burst out between nation and nation. Each Italian city is a nation. The surrounding province has been constituted for many centuries without any rationalized gerrymandering of the sort attempted by the Constituent Assembly of France in 1790. Save four or five prefectures concocted by the Fascists, every Italian province has been a territorial unit since Roman times. We may say that they are part of the interior life of every Italian. So is the supreme, unwritten law of federation which bound them together in the days of primitive Roman liberty. Except, of course, for the rare artificial boundaries drawn by the Fascists, the provincial limits still correspond to those of the ancient Roman *civitates*.

In truth the Italians are the most particularist of the great peoples of Europe. But they are such because they feel that for them this entails no risk, since their national unity has proved immovable throughout centuries of trial.

CHAPTER II

Why Their History Has Made the Italians
Discontented Internationalists

STICKLERS for particular rights we are, indeed, and sticklers for unity just as certainly, but above all we Italians are the most universalist of European peoples. From this comes the deep humanity of our great men, from Dante and Aquinas to Mazzini, and also the key to certain defects in Italian political thought. Whatever decent element fascism managed in a distant past to attract has promised, or hoped, to repair these defects. But those who tried to get rid of the universalist side of Italian character through artificial stimulation of nationalist passions succeeded only in obscuring one of the noblest sides of our nature without putting anything noble or healthy in its place.

True, the universalist character of our political thinking has often hindered us gravely when action was needed. How else can we explain—taking the most famous example— why the author of the *Divine Comedy*, who lived in the richest years of Italy's history, filled his poem with lament, regret for the past and anathema for the present? From Flanders to Constantinople, Florence and her bankers dominated Dante's Europe. Genoa and Venice ruled the seas. Every Italian city had cathedrals and spires which were among the marvels of the world. Italy's religious life had produced Francis of Assisi. Its poetry surpassed the Provençal by leaps and bounds even before Petrarch and

Boccaccio. But all this was as nothing to Dante, for the political unity of Christendom had been broken, and now that the Roman emperor lived beyond the Alps, Italy was no longer the "garden of the Empire."

Other minds, less luminous but fully as sincere, agreed with Dante. When Giovanni Villani the chronicler looked at Florence he could do nothing but "fear the wrath of God." Another Villani saw about him "only grave dangers of division." "Semper Lombardia in malo stato fuit" echoed the lamenting *Chronica Astensis:* Lombardy has ever been in a sad way.

Two centuries later, during the *cinquecento,* this dissatisfaction began to sound like the Hebrew prophets; and not without reason. For one thing, the "Italiane tempeste," as one of the Villani called them, had become more painful since the foreign invasion. For another, all the great writers of the sixteenth century, being true sons of the Renaissance, were if possible more keenly aware of the distance between their Italy and the ideal of the Pax Romana than their predecessors had been. Historians like Machiavelli loved Italy much, but not one of them chose to mention from the pages of the old chronicles the story of that matchless day in 1170 when millions of Italians—priests, mutes, and blind men being alone excepted—went to their baptismal fonts to swear this oath:

In the name of God, amen. I swear by the Gospel that I shall not make peace, truce, or treaty with the Emperor Frederick or with his son or with his wife or any other person of his name, either directly or through another; and in good faith, by every means within my power, I shall do my best to hinder any army great or small, German or of any other land belonging to the Emperor beyond the Alps, from entering Italy; and if an army does enter, I shall wage active war upon the Emperor and all his followers until that army shall be gone from Italy; and when my sons reach the age of fourteen I shall have them swear a like oath.

The result was the battle of Legnano, one of the brightest pages in the history of the new peoples of Europe and their struggle for liberty. That the victory achieved nothing permanent may be imputed to the universalist aspect of our character. The Italians kept their word; they beat the German king who was so intent on the rape of their rights and privileges. But as soon as this German began talking in his decrees about his hereditary right to the splendors of Rome, the Italian mind gave in.

This also explains the character of the wars which the Italians have supported. Never could the Lombard League make up its mind to prevent an Emperor from coming down from the Alps; never did they pursue him beyond the Brenner Pass after his defeat. Thus the Germans could pick their own time to come through the Alpine passes "cum omni pace" to pounce without warning on the lush fields of the Po. Beaten, they could take refuge beyond the Alps. The danger was always great for the Italian cities, while almost negligible for the Germans once they had discovered that the Italians were content simply to defend themselves. The stupid legend about Italy's lack of military courage is the work of picayune historians. If they only knew it, what they are talking about is really a collective moral superiority, which if it had been wider spread in the world of that time would have made a healthier Europe.

A few years after Legnano, in 1179, work was begun on the canal of the Tessino, on the plains where the battle had taken place. For that time, the project was enormous. And the canal of the Muzza, until the end of the nineteenth century the largest in Europe, was opened after another battle, at Casorate, against another Emperor, Frederick II, in 1239. At that time a hundred Italian cities wrote into their statutes the law which permitted free passage for any brook, however small, that brought water, even across seigneurial lands, to the lone field of the humblest villager. Outside Italy landholders with touchy feelings on the subject of absolute property rights were until very recently successful in fighting such laws. At about the same time, moreover, Bologna led Europe in releasing all serfs from the land, and all the serfs, men and women, were redeemed by the Comune and set free, the landlords being allowed to keep only their property.

One lone Italian historian, Carlo Cattaneo, thought to bring such facts as these to light. But his sovereignly independent mind was Federalist-Republican, sandwiched between the Unification-Monarchist Cavour and the Unification-Republican Mazzini. This fact guaranteed Cattaneo's obscurity. To serve a losing cause is a great wrong in the eyes of history, that purblind prostitute; that is why Cattaneo is practically unknown.[1]

Nineteenth-century Italian historians disdained even the acts of military valor that they saw with their own eyes. What difference to them, since the eyes of Italy were watching "Its sovereign empire fallen to the depths," as Giovanni

---

[1] Before his exile to the United States the Italian historian Salvemini wrote an essay, admirable for its clarity and powerful synthesis, as preface to an anthology of Cattaneo's work. For the same series I had done a volume on Mazzini. On orders from the Fascists the publisher was obliged to withdraw the two volumes, which thus went out of print in Italy. What we do not know is whether this was done out of hate for the two great Italians or for the compilers.

Guidiccioni lamented in a sonnet every Italian knew by heart?

The main artisan of the French victory in Italy was the Italian Trivulzio, a mortal enemy of the Sforza house. It was Trivulzio who discovered a new passage for artillery through the Alps; on the opposite side, it was another Italian, Prospero Colonna, who with his army surprised the French Lautrec in Milan.

When Brescia rose against the French, nine knights had sworn to free their city or die. The French put down the revolt, but the nine knights died fighting in the streets. Only one, Fenarolo, escaped with a wound. When they found him hiding in a tomb, he sank his knife into his neck. They carried him to the castle and promised pardon if he would talk. He tore open his wound with his own hands and died.

Again at Brescia a short time afterward, when the Venetians were definitely beaten, the brothers Lorenzo and Ludovico Porcellaga turned their horses and charged the French chiefs. Ludovico was killed instantly; Lorenzo fought on alone until he fell on the body of his brother. Respecting such courage, Gaston de Foix ordered his men not to kill him, but Lorenzo continued to resist until he shared his brother's fate. That evening Gaston de Foix accompanied the two bodies to the cathedral and standing before the coffins declared to his knights that their duty was to preserve the memory of such pure heroism.

Siena withstood the longest and bloodiest siege of the sixteenth century. Pestilence, famine, and the artillery of Charles V reduced the most exquisite city of Tuscany to a shadow. Monluc wrote of these people, whom Dante had called frivolous, that they defended their liberty with the courage of knights of the Round Table and that their women were as brave as his bravest men. After the capitulation the few Sienese who survived withdrew from the city to their old dependency, Montalcino, where again they made a stand against the Imperials who had taken up the pursuit after a short truce. Here also the women fought beside the men. The day they surrendered they burned the standard of the Republic and the dies that had minted the money of free Siena. A volume could be filled with similar instances, but every great Italian historian has disdained them. Even today they are known only to a handful of provincial scholars.

The age when these things happened was one of invasion and shame. Like Michelangelo in his famous quatrain, generations of men repeated:

> Sweet is my sleep, but more to be mere stone
> So long as ruin and dishonor reign;
> To bear nought, to feel nought is my great gain;
> Then wake me not. Speak in an undertone.[2]

After the depressing Spanish occupation of the seventeenth century, Italy produced a movement of political and social ideas which ran throughout the whole *settecento*. Well before the shock of the French Revolution the nineteenth century was already astir. Beccaria's immortal treatise, *Of Crimes and Punishments*, sent a wave of reform from Milan to Naples, abolishing torture, eliminating exemption from taxation, replacing fetid medieval prisons with houses of correction. With half of these Turgot could have saved the French monarchy. But in one respect the rich, magnanimous generation of the *Risorgimento* followed in the steps of the

[2] *The Sonnets of Michelangelo Buonarotti*, translated by John Addington Symonds, Portland, Me.: Mosher, 1895, p. cix.

great *cinquecento* classics: they missed seeing the worth of their eighteenth-century predecessors. Since the *settecento* had worked no miracles, they overlooked it.

In 1860 the unification of Italy crowned the heroic *Risorgimento*. Yet, while in Italy men had conspired and died, England and France achieved their great economic and cultural advance of the first half of the nineteenth century. Any unprejudiced person must admit Croce's luminous demonstration, in his recent *History of Contemporary Italy*, that the ground which Italy had consequently to cover between 1860 and 1920 was formidable, indeed. Yet the result left the Italians dissatisfied. Their ideals and hopes had been too high and vast to be attained in less than a century of liberty.

CHAPTER III

And Why This Discontent Has Produced the Principal Defect of a Part of the Italian Middle Class: Fustian

THIS NOBLE and disinterested discontent has always produced among mediocre Italians a tendency toward bombast about the Roman Empire. When this gets the upper hand we know that we may expect a period of intellectual and political decline. This allegedly proud summons back to *Romanità* is rehashed at every opportunity by windy poets who appropriate the heritage of the Caesars and show foreigners the ruins of Rome as though they held a mortgage on the world. It all ends by stirring in us a sadness generally associated with the sight of confetti the morning after the ball. Or else we smile as at the drums which simulate off-stage thunder at Punch and Judy shows.

The finest centuries of our history looked back, not to the conquests of the Caesars, but to the universal idea of the Empire, with Rome and Italy at its center, based upon equal rights. Leibnitz says in the Preface of his *Codex diplomaticus* that in the Middle Ages the emperor and the pope were the twin heads of the Christian Republic. The Italians were the first to become aware that they agreed on this point. Between the twelfth and the fourteenth centuries the Italian soul assumed its final form, and has never since lost its desire for universality. The cruel glories of Rome were far less instrumental in its formation.

For the medieval Italians, the Roman who meant most was, not an emperor, but Virgil—a poet transformed into a combination of oriental and semi-Christian sage. The one popular emperor was Trajan the Just; his closest rival, Justinian, really belonged to the new times.

In the period following the Counter Reformation in Italy, when formalism killed enthusiasm and the schools were standardized under the Jesuits, Rome inspired much current literature; but it was a Rome sugared into something like the Roman paintings of Panini. Writers and teachers of the seventeenth and eighteenth centuries chose their heroes among the Romans rather than among the men of the Middle Ages, because they felt that Rome was less dangerous. They shelved Tacitus, because his love of liberty might be contagious. And the clumsy Roman decorum which the Jesuit schools admired meant nothing but pretension and distrust of what is natural.

The last and most eloquent Italian to be bewitched by this artificial, stylized Rome was Carlo Botta, whose voluminous *History of Italy* was famous at the beginning of the nineteenth century and is still to be found in our old country houses beside the *Consulate and Empire* of Thiers. For Botta the golden age of Italy and of the world was the era of the Roman Empire. The Middle Ages seemed to him only a "desolate time, especially in Italy," in which "ignorance, force, and barbarity" predominated. Botta was the last sincere admirer of Imperial Rome. The *Risorgimento* began with a galaxy of noteworthy individuals who emerged in every region between Piedmont and Sicily and in every field of endeavor, not even excluding that of historical studies. Because of the ideas and books of these men the devotion to the grandeur that was Rome was thrown aside like an outworn garment. One of these authors, Micali, even went so far, in his *Italia avanti il dominio dei Romani*, as to maintain that Rome had never been other than a brute force which had clipped the wings of the Italian spirit just as it was starting to rise out of the happy union of the different peoples of the peninsula.

Romanticism helped these men to turn toward the Middle Ages as toward a sanctified and afflicted era whence the genuine, living Italian people had emerged. Our bourgeoisie and our working class were moved by the preaching of Mazzini to recognize themselves as descendants of the communes of the twelfth and thirteenth centuries, struggling against the German emperors.

It is true that at the same time, parallel to the old Italian tradition of anticlericalism, another current drew its hero lore from the ancient heritage of the Ghibellines of the time of Frederick II. But their tradition did not go back to *Romanità*; their roots also were sunk in the Middle Ages.

The nineteenth century, liberal and democratic in Italy as elsewhere, felt more or less keenly that even from the point of view of art the Roman Empire had never been anything but a triumph of mass brutality. "Colossal" was as much the watchword in Imperial Rome as it was in the Germany of William II. Italians realized that the great edifices of Rome were symbols of the impoverishment and depopulation which beset the peninsula and opened the way to the incursions of the German tribes.

The dull self-satisfaction and complacent pride in Imperial Rome which are apparent in Italy during her decadent periods remind us of the Rome which under Hadrian minted money bearing slogans such as *Italia felix* and *Temporum felicitas*. To be so smug one must be either blind or decadent. The disconcerting lesson which the history of Italy gives the world is that times of violent civil strife and antagonism between *popolo grasso* and *popolo minuto* are precisely the times of greatest perfection in poetry, painting, and sculpture, of great enterprises in exploration, finance, and world-dominating commerce. The truest and most lasting words that Machiavelli ever spoke were these: "The multitude is more constant and wiser than the monarch," and "Those who condemn the struggle between the patricians and the plebians condemn the primary cause of the grandeur of Rome; they attach more importance to the noise of the struggle than to its benefits."

The last Italian writer for whom *Romanità* was neither a tool nor an artifice was Carducci, the spokesman of the generation of 1870–90. Like Machiavelli in his histories, Carducci took his principal, most intimate inspiration from his love of country, and the symbols of his ideal from republican Rome. So also did Leopardi,[1] but our greatest modern poet was such a universalist that his love of country gradually melted into a more broadly human sentiment; he did not relinquish his love of Italy, but broadened it. Carducci's inability to do this explains why, despite the power and beauty of his lyric work, he has not been taken up outside Italy. A sort of justice rules the fame of poets.

Fate was cruel to Carducci in his old age. This honest, steadfast man had tried to serve his country by offering her a single ideal which rose above factions, *Romanità*.

[1] "My native land, I do the walls behold . . ." *The Poems of Leopardi*, translated by G. L. Blickerstreth, Cambridge, the University Press, 1923, p. 137.

He did not foresee that in impure hands his art would disguise sterility and that even his patriotism, so genuine in him, would mask vain redundance and theatrical trumpery. Was not D'Annunzio clever enough to proclaim himself "Carducci's son"? D'Annunzio's work is the complete antithesis of everything the good and faithful Carducci venerated.

At the beginning of the fascist years, in which Italy has seemed to repudiate the most authentic of her traditions, Mussolini and his accomplices brought forth all the inventions à la D'Annunzio; they did not contribute anything original, even in that morbid field.

In the seventeenth and eighteenth centuries the Jesuit school-masters and the sonneteers took their spurious inspiration from Roman history. Metastasio is the best specimen of the type. In the crisis which came upon Italy after the first World War the petty bourgeois failures among the teachers, the liberal professions, and the public services were victims of a new attack of rhetorical fustian, of which D'Annunzio had been the harbinger. Despite its tragic atmosphere, the first World War itself revealed how far D'Annunzian grandiloquence had extended its ravages. Happily it was then reserved for special occasions. Ten years later, with the advent of fascism, it became a component of everyday life. I still keep letters from Italian generals I knew on the Italian and Macedonian fronts. They are short and common sense, sometimes caustic, the very picture of the men who wrote them—sensible, retiring, shy men, like most generals everywhere. But as soon as the same officers sat down to write an order of the day they felt obliged to present it in turgid prose. They felt that there was a special style appropriate for such routine.

It must be said that the same was true in France during the Revolution. Almost all the members of the National Convention and the Jacobins had been crammed at school with Roman heroes. They could rid themselves of a king, but not of a "noble" style such as their eighteenth-century masters had inculcated in them. When they wrote home to their families their letters were lively and simple, like those of my generals in Macedonia; but when they bestrode the Roman hobbyhorse, they were unbearable—at no time has Italy carried it so far. The pseudo-Roman style became habitual with all "patriots." Every short-order cook became a Brutus, whereas in Italy the people have never been corrupted by pompous bombast, not even under fascism. During the perturbed years between the two world wars and even more after 1939 when the dictators extended their war over most of Europe, the common man was never taken in by this grandiloquence. The small bourgeois and the white-collar class furnished from the very start the blindest, most enthusiastic Nazis and Fascists.

For these unfortunates, crammed to the ears with the Roman Empire, the miraculous beauty of medieval Italy —which is beautiful as life is, and as disorderly—could only be incomprehensible, just as they found the nobility of the generation of the *Risorgimento* incomprehensible. Their spiritual ancestors are men like Cola di Rienzo, the poor rhetoric-jobber of the fourteenth century whose morbid vanity led him to bathe in a red marble basin where he was told the Emperors had bathed.

But perhaps foreigners should leave to those Italians whose patriotism has remained clear-sighted and humane the task of criticizing the other Italians who took for their model the period which was really the decadence of a complete civilization and whose disappearance permitted a new Italy, richer and fuller in spite of its disorder, to blossom forth. All in all, I am sometimes tempted to find excuses for certain aspects of fascist stupidity, when I imagine what other European peoples might have done had they been able to boast, as we were, of the heritage of the Caesars. At least I am so tempted when I consider the pretensions that so many Germans base upon a Holy Roman Empire which was neither holy nor an empire, nor Roman.

CHAPTER IV

The Italians and Their Literature

ITALIAN LITERATURE is unique in that it attained formal perfection at the very beginning, when it produced its most universal genius, Dante, and with him Petrarch and Boccaccio. Shakespeare, Racine, and Goethe appeared only after generations of English, French, and German poetry. In Italy, Guido Guinicelli and Guido Cavalcanti had scarcely time to dazzle the thirteenth century with their *canzoni* and *ballate*, which caused the old troubadours to be forgotten, when the sovereign poet arrived "che l'uno e l'altro caccera di nido." Dante did indeed "drive the one and the other from the nest," but Dante is Dante and stands by himself. Next after him are Petrarch and Boccaccio, each alone of his kind.

Boccaccio reveals the Italian soul of his time and probably of all times. But poets like Dante and Petrarch, and, after the Renaissance, Ariosto and Tasso, speak for themselves and through themselves to the universal conscience. The same is true of the nineteenth-century Leopardi. Dante is indeed full of Italian passions, and Petrarch thanks God that he was born an Italian. But they no more speak for Italy than Racine speaks for France or Cervantes for Spain or Whitman for the United States. For every genuine poet his fatherland, although vital to his interior life, is only part of a wider world. A poet who is only national is not a true poet. Manzoni, for example, loved and served Italy.

But he must have thought of himself when he wrote of
Homer, "Argos claims him at the expense of Athens, and
Rhodes contends with Smyrna for his citizenship"—to
which he adds, "And he knows no other country than
heaven." Dante himself, Italian though he was, declares
that "the world in general" is his country and replies to
intermediaries who want him to end his exile by accepting
humiliating conditions: "Can I not contemplate the light
of sun and stars anywhere? Can I not anywhere meditate
the supreme truths?"

The game of finding the soul of a country in its poets is
futile. It is just as vain to speak of a Dantesque Italy as of
a Shakespearian England or a Racinian France. On the contrary, universal poets are those who exert an influence on
the sentiments and the aspirations of successive generations.
All Italians are brought up to worship Dante, and Dante
has influenced them much more than Shakespeare has the
English or Racine the French. The densest Italian has at
some time been moved by these lines, some of Dante's
endecasillabi, wherein thought and images are more rapid
and sharp than in any other poem. American nurses with
the Expeditionary Force of 1917 have told me that con-
valescent soldiers of Italian origin asked so frequently for
a volume of Dante that several hundred copies had to be
purchased. Neither the English nor the French have anything like our Dante worship. And too many Germans have
gone to Goethe only for a justification for pride "from
the German standpoint," faithless here as elsewhere to the
poet who preached that they should rise to the level of
universal minds. In Italy, Dante has become a national al-
tar where everyone takes communion, or at least pretends

to. The fact is that Dante has been adopted by century after century as a measure of Italian sentiment; in the *Divine Comedy* there are even those "natural frontiers" which the French have sought in history and geography, but which their poets have never provided. When I was campaigning in the Italian parliament for a program of amicable understanding with our newly liberated Slavic neighbors, my assertion was that the annexation of a part of Dalmatia, 95 percent populated by Slavs who intended to stay Slavs, would be in no way profitable to Italy. A purely Dantesque argument carried great weight both with the elite and with the masses. Did not Dante exclude Dalmatia from Italy when he said that the gulf of Quarnero shuts off Italy and washes her frontiers?

At the lowest ebb in her history, the seventeenth and eighteenth centuries, Italy abandoned Dante. There were more editions of the *Divine Comedy* between 1815 and 1848, the age of the *Risorgimento,* than during the two hundred years preceding.

One may wonder whether the unequaled perfection of Dante, at the beginning of our literature, and the art of Petrarch whose lyricism is still so very close to our hearts, have not been the original causes of the exclusively bookish formation of most of our poets. They had too many imposing examples to look back to. It was more simple and natural for Villon to find his inspiration in his own soul or for an English poet to be inspired by nature. The Italian knew the *Inferno* and most of the *canzoni* of Petrarch by heart. Was this a handicap? The fact is that for Italians our classics were long more than mere masterworks. They constituted the ideal fatherland which foreign overlords could not conquer. They promised glory and liberty for the future.

Only the Chinese have made their classics such a substantial base of national consciousness. But whereas the Chinese have never offered anything but passive resistance —like the rubber ball which gives to any pressure and loses the marks again when released—for our fathers the Italian classics implied not only consciousness but active resistance also. The traditional Chinese man of letters never seems to have a beating, suffering heart. Veneration of an august poetic past made the sons of Ham believe that literary style is a sort of mystery and the privilege of a caste. Everything has been reduced to formula. Even today the Chinese generals, loyal ones and traitors in Japanese pay alike, issue proclamations in which the same old characters reproduce the same old hemistichs of some poet or other of the Sung dynasty.

When I was minister to China, Guido Vitale, a Sinologist attached to the Italian legation, published a charming collection of Chinese popular poems. The literati of Peking wondered whether he had not gone mad, and the great and mighty Prince Pu-Lung, who did me the honor of being my friend, warned me against the lunacy of my secretary. In Prince Pu-Lung I saw a living example of our fifteenth-century Italian humanists—those who regretted that Dante, "that great genius," had stooped to write in Italian whereas he could have given new masterpieces to the Latin tongue.

In the long stream of our literature there are two currents, which mingle without mixing. One is expressed by Dante, in the following words.

Quando
Amor mi spira, nota
("When love inspires me, I write.")

This type has come down as far as Leopardi and Manzoni. The other consists of those whose cleverness produces
bookstall successes, sometimes astonishing, like the works
of Vincenzo Monti, but who are too often uninspired.

When liberty is lost and artificial orderliness reigns in
streets and books, literary originality abandons Italy. The
field is open for Roman eagles and arches of Constantine
and also for women whose exquisite words never seem to
reach the heart. The Dori, the Fili, and the Ebes of the
stifling age of Spanish influence are neither Italian nor universal. Our poetry came to life only at the beginning of the
Risorgimento, with Manzoni and Leopardi. The reinless
passion and the excessive suffering of Leopardi brought
Dante back to us. It was Leopardi himself who wrote, in
full consciousness of his own genius, that from the sixteenth century down to his own there had been "verse, but
no poetry." Manzoni and Leopardi left behind them not
only personal followers but also converts to simplicity, sincerity, in brief to true poetry.

During my long visits to France I have often felt that
behind the attitudes of some cultivated *républicain* were
the hundred and fifty volumes of Voltaire, kept like a jewel
in the family library. Similarly, I have felt in more austere
Frenchmen the prolonged and almost religious reading of
Pascal. In Italy it is different. Not our literature, but our
history, so tragic and so full of heights and depths, explains our characters. Our classic literature was born to
perfection, nursed by the perfection of Latin, in the

shadow of Dante. Because of this, literature quickly became remote from our people except in the supreme masterworks.

From Dante's time to our own the true life of Italy has been more like the turbulence of Greece than the official rigidity of Rome. (I am neglecting here, of course, the vain show of the fascist years. They are only a brief interlude of unreality.) Our noisy and agitated municipal life, yesterday the audacity of merchants and navigators opening the trade routes of the world, today these same qualities appearing in our emigrants, the spirit of faction, the originality of individual temperaments, all these are far more reminiscent of the Ionian cities than of joyless Roman decorum.

But this typically Italian turbulence is disparaged by our classic writers. Our story-tellers are the only ones who delight in it with happy and tranquil sincerity. Boccaccio's *Decameron* still teems with ageless Italians. During his *trecento* the pomp of the church is superb, but faith is weak, seemingly burned out with the fine flame of Saint Francis in the preceding century. Dante thunders against "new people and sudden wealth," but Boccaccio belongs to the new people and speaks for them. He likes to live among them. Like all Italians he has known since childhood about the visions and legends which followed the year 1000, but his Tuscan smile has not left his lips. His balanced tranquility makes him sovereignly tolerant of all human wretchedness, and his indulgence is equally impartial toward the public market and the Church, the hovel and the palace of the great.

Dante sometimes describes in a line the types we meet

in daily life, like the old tailor struggling to thread his needle ("Come vecchio sartor fa nella cruna"). But we feel that his soul reaches out only to tragic lovers like Paolo and Francesca or to unbending heroes like Farinata. When Boccaccio writes about these princes, knights, and ladies, his world becomes pallidly conventional, whereas his scenes swarm with life when he writes about merchants, artists, and peasants. It is in Boccaccio—despite the latinate rhythm of his language—and in other story-tellers like him, that one may follow the long and authentic scenario of Italian adventure and sentiment.

The French *conteurs* of the fifteenth and sixteenth centuries are no more inventive or realistic than their *trouvère* predecessors. Almost always we have the same betrayed husband and the same sprightly wife who plagues both husband and lover. . . . Even Lafontaine, whose amiable genius lays bare human nature to us, does not provide us with scenes of French life. With the Italian *conteurs*, however, it is as if our own people were taking revenge for the often over-abstract solemnity of standard literature. Everything is the direct echo of the life of the people, in prose fiction as in such popular poetry as the *rispetto* of Tuscany, the Neapolitan *arietta*, and the Sicilian *canzuna*.

Like the spontaneous Sicilian *ottava*, the Italian tale rarely shines brilliantly. Boccaccio's stories are the only ones which hold our interest in a situation or a final phrase which illumines the whole tale with its stroke of wit.

French and German tales are semi-mythological in origin. In Italy the stories rapidly grew up about human types who lived in the time of the story-tellers; such types as Arlotto, the priest from the vicinity of fifteenth-century

Florence who is still famous today, or Gonella, the clown of the court of Ferrara. Another difference between the Italian story and that of the other countries reveals an essentially national trait. In the French and German *fabliaux*—and only yesterday in the Norman tales of Maupassant—the single aim of the farce is to obtain a material advantage or to enjoy a material pleasure. But the *facezie* of Arlotto and of the innumerable others who followed him are devoid of immediate interest. The authors sometimes even try to destroy that interest. What they have in view is to satisfy self-esteem. This trait is still one of the most vital in present-day Italian character, if you know where to look for it beneath the pompous exterior of the fascist tragi-comedy.

Their amiable tolerance helps our chroniclers through most of their psychological problems. In the one case where they are unjust, they are extremely Italian. Their patriotism is twofold: pride and love for Italy, but also deep if hidden affection for their native city. Thus each time even the skeptical Boccaccio himself puts on the stage a thief, a hypocrite, or a forger, he cannot bring himself to make the rogue a Florentine, but assigns him to Milan or Naples. Four centuries later we find the same patriotism, for Venice this time, in Goldoni. His typical liar comes from Naples, his boaster and his miser from other Italian regions.

It is only in these story-tellers that we find faithfully reproduced one of the deepest-grounded traits of the Italian people, such as they have become from centuries of silent struggle against the mighty and against nature—a sort of philosophy, at once resigned and gently nonchalant, which strikes the superficial observer as an almost oriental fatalism, but is in hard fact the fruit of a bitter familiarity with history, combined with a daily, practical effort, silent and untiring, to eliminate the effects of evil.

Here, taken from Franco Sacchetti, is one of a thousand possible examples. A peasant from Decomano went to complain to Francesco de' Medici that one of the latter's relatives wanted to take his vine plot from him. This is the way he ended his complaint:

You must know, since you know life so well, that in the world we live in everything depends on *the way things happen.* One time we happen to have chicken pox, another time we happen to get the plague. Yesterday the wine happened to go bad; tomorrow no one can get justice; another time, it just happens that we go out and shoot each other. Sure . . . it's the way things happen that makes one damned thing after another. And I know there's no protection against all that. That's why I ask you only one thing. If it's the way things happen that makes people go around taking other people's vine plots, why all right, let your relative take mine, and God's blessing go with him, because I can't do anything against the way things happen. But if it just happens not to be the reason that people go around taking vine plots, I ask you very urgently not to let my vine plot be taken away.

All through Italian history one can find not only stories but also histories written with this sharpness. But the greatness of the giants on one hand and the fancy windiness of the mediocrities on the other have hidden them. Almost every city has chronicles as exquisitely fresh and spontaneous as that of Fra Salimbene of Parma. But the world has been dazzled and repelled at the same time by the disciplined beauty of the great historians of the *cinquecento:* Guicciardini, Giambullari, Varchi, Davanzati.

The life of the first great Italian prose master, Boccaccio, is the first great example of this eternal mistake. He spent the best years of his youth on poems and treatises stuffed with mythology and Roman history. Dante's influence was too much for him. Boccaccio tried to imitate him as Dante had tried to imitate Virgil, and he wrote an immortal book, the *Decameron,* only when he had forgotten his learned impedimenta and his dreams of glory. The fate of art in Italy has too often been that of Boccaccio—it has been affected and over-ornate when writers have been dominated only by respect and veneration for their great predecessors. This is why one is so much more aware of the simple, genuine, everyday Italian soul in the relatively obscure story-tellers and chroniclers than in the pages signed by famous names. This is also why after the long sleep of the seventeenth century the breach between literature and the people became so wide. Since literature had become detached from life, Italians felt more at home with lower-class story-tellers, whether they wrote in Italian or in dialect.

As a child I remember seeing the peasants on their way to market in the neighboring city to buy the four-penny stories of the most enduringly successful of the popular yarn-spinners, Giulio Cesare della Croce. Della Croce was a locksmith of Bologna, father of fourteen children, who spent his evenings writing to add to his meager income. He popularized the stories of Bertoldo, clown of King Alboin of the Longobards, and of his son Bertoldino. Thanks to Giulio Cesare della Croce the agile knavery of Bertoldo has become part and parcel of our folklore.

When they banished Bertoldo from Longobard ground,

he came riding home again immediately in a cart, covered with earth from another state; when they forebade him to appear at court, he presented himself there without appearing, hidden under a collander; and when they condemned him to death, he asked but one boon, to be allowed to choose the tree from which he should hang, and after twenty years of search at the King's expense, he had still not found a tree to suit him.

In Tuscany—the very homeland of refined taste—our great poets long remained as much part of the living literature as the tellers of folk tales; and even yet, in the long winter evenings men sit by the hearth listening for hours to the peasant who reads aloud the songs of Tasso or of Ariosto. Time was—in the fourteenth century—when the same was true of the *Divine Comedy:* everyone read it and needed no learned notes, at least for the human episodes. And the clerks scarcely needed them for the theological and ethical allusions. That was the time when men knew by instinct what Francesco de Sanctis dared tell his pupils at the University of Naples between 1871 and 1877: "When you find places where Dante is unclear, skip them. In those he isn't Dante."

It was the fault of the writers—in poetry and prose both —that they fell under the influence of the Spanish and lost the esteem of the common people. They kept their vogue, even outside Italy, only among the great. Theirs was the time of the pompous, windy style. They wrote peans for the victories of the Catholic Powers over the Crescent, even the somewhat seedy triumphs of the Knights of the Order of Saint Stefano over a few ketch loads of Musselman pirates. Or else they wrote of the Virgin, Magdalen and

her tresses, patriotic songs without a country, sacred songs
without religious sentiment, love songs without tenderness
or passion—in brief a repertory of admirable technical
brilliance, dry as dust with respect to love, or Christian
faith, or love of country. Let us take for an example of
patriotism the sonnet of Filicaja with its too famous line
which our fathers all knew by heart: "Ah, wert thou
stronger or less beautiful."

It is addressed to an Italy that never was on sea or land,
an Italy, as we are well aware, produced by the same
literary conventions which produced the "candid bosoms"
of beauties which never breathed a living breath. The
more Filicaja in his pomp reproaches Italy for not using
her strength and the more he talks of foreign enemies who
were once our serfs, the surer we are that these are only
literary calisthenics. The good Filicaja is shaken by identical frenzies when he sings the glories of the king of Poland or the king of Spain.

The language itself, once so nakedly lucid, became remote from the people. Even in the formulae of everyday
life it did not escape bombast. Up to the sixteenth century
every Italian letter ended with a simple "state sano" (keep
well) or, if someone wanted to exaggerate a bit, "tutto
vostro" (entirely yours). It was after the arrival of the
Spaniards and the subsequent change of manners that the
simple second person forms "tu" and "voi" were replaced
by the pompous "Lei" and "Ella," referring to a "Vostra
Signoria" expressed or understood. "Signoria" was quickly
joined in polite language by "Eccellenza" and "Magni-
ficenza." And finally at the end of letters one came to
"kiss the hands of your Lordship," after centuries of be-

ing content with the mere "state sano." We must add, however, that the Italians did not adopt certain extreme Spanish fashions, like the "kissing your lordship's feet," whence the initials Q.B.S.P. at the end of letters even in twentieth-century Spain.

But we would be falling into the narrow nationalism of Filicaja if we tried to pin on Spain alone the responsibility for the hispanomania which infected Italy for two centuries. The truth is that Italy and Spain were subject to a common fate, which in a period of common decadence was more immediately visible in us than in the Spanish only because the Spaniards could hide their trouble longer under the cover of a powerful, tightly knit state. The decadence of the two countries was essentially the same; both peoples were victims of a medieval opposition to the political reforms which stirred the north of Europe and assured the north a long period, not really of intellectual superiority, but of social and spiritual preponderance.

Yet despite the suffocating atmosphere and the fact that the literati had distinctly lost any savor, Italy gave the world—like flashes in the dark—thinkers like Galileo, Campanella, and Vico. This is what explains our miraculous awakening at the end of the eighteenth century and the beginning of the nineteenth, with Beccaria, Leopardi, and Manzoni.

· CHAPTER V

The Italians and Their Dialects

MEANWHILE, how could the soul of the people express itself, now that its literary mandarins had stuffed their language with conceits?

The Italian people no longer sang or made love in the classic language. They sang, they made love, only in the dialects. They became like conspirators using a cipher in a period of political oppression. As long as the Italian language kept its vigor there was dialect literature only at the extremities of the peninsula, in Venice and Sicily. But when literature fell to the level of the Filicajas and Chiabreras the dialects came to life and took their revenge everywhere. In every city poets rose as if by enchantment —and they wrote with thirty different accents. Popular poetry and comedy boldly seized on the Italy—its manners, its hatreds, its traditions, its loves—which the orthodox men of letters had contemptuously ignored.

Here, then, is one of the paradoxes of Italian life. Everywhere else in Europe dialect literatures had been only groping experiments, quickly superseded by national literatures, when, as in France, the Bossuets and the Racines set the tone. Only in Italy did the dialects come in after an age of unusual literary brilliance; as soon as the standard literature went to sleep, they took over. They satisfied an old Italian taste. Punchinello, who dominates the Neapolitan stage, is probably the Maccus of the Roman bas-reliefs: in him one glimpses the spirit of a people whose heritage is Greek as well as Byzantine, Roman, Norman, and Spanish. A mere servant? Possibly! But he is *servo di due padroni* [1] (the servant of two masters) and seeks, between the two, the way to liberty.

Italian writers have too often spoken of the *Commedia dell'arte* as of a low episode in our cultural history. Actually Punchinello at Naples and Harlequin at Venice— not to speak of Brighella, Stenterello, Captain Fracassa, and Pantaloon—reveal the secrets of popular life and manners far more fully than do the literary exercises of the seventeenth and eighteenth centuries. In these there is nothing but fine sentiment, which too rarely comes from the heart. In the *Commedia dell'arte,* and in a good share of the dialect poetry, only the vulgar side of life is exposed, because it is the funny side. Dreams, delicacies, inner loyalties—these are unexpressed, but we often feel them beneath the surface.

Goldoni once sent Voltaire one of his comedies, and Voltaire—always a little the flatterer when people flattered him—replied with one of the snap judgments to which he was prone: "What purity! You have rescued your country from the hands of the Harlequins." But Goldoni knew his own debt to the Harlequins; all his life he continued to turn out comedies not only in Italian but also in the Venetian patois, which he filled with smiling, intelligent Harlequins.

While Italian literature had its greatest geniuses right at the very beginning, the dialects produced their best poets only at the end of their popularity. These were Carlo Porta at Milan and Gioachino Belli at Rome.

[1] The title of a famous Italian popular comedy.—Translator.

It was when Bonaparte's French burst upon Milan that Porta appeared and made his reputation. One day he was a little, unknown clerk; on the next all Lombardy knew his verses by heart. Today the types he invented are part of the heritage of all Italy, almost like certain characters in the *Divine Comedy* or Don Abbondio of *The Betrothed*. His Marchioness Travasa has given her name to all the titled old ladies who thank God for the blue blood that runs in their veins. And Italians feel about his popular hero— Giovannin Bongee—as Spaniards do about Sancho Panza.

Porta appeared in Milan with the French Revolution; Belli arrived in Rome with the Restoration after Waterloo. The Roman dialect is very close to Italian—so close indeed that to suggest a perfect pronunciation of our language, we say: "Tuscan speech in a Roman mouth." Porta had trouble hiding his indignation against the nobles, the French invader, the worldly *abbés,* and the too tractable common folk like Giovannin Bongee and *Marchionn di gambavert,* but Belli—a poet above all—never seemed to lose his temper. It was without the least apparent trace of indignation that he pilloried the petty favor seekers of the papal court and the parasites attached to the cardinals and the Roman princes. Each of his sonnets was a masterpiece. Porta has not been translated because he is not translatable, but why has no one translated Belli into French, German, Spanish, and English? Like the Europe of today, the Rome of Belli's time did not even suspect the power of his sonnets; Italy discovered him only after 1870. The indifferent Rome of his day had asked him the same question that Cardinal Ippolito d'Este asked Aristo: "Ah, Messer Lodovico, where do you find so much nonsense to say?"

The "nonsense" of Belli, like that of Porta, was Italian genius itself, which often pillaged the dialects to enrich the language. For example, French contains thousands of very short words which rhyme so subtly that the rhyme seems almost veiled. This is even more true of English. Italian, however, is sharper and harsher. Admirable for expressing ideas, it is much less musical—despite the legend to the contrary. The dialects, on the other hand, have as many short words as French or English, whence the unobtrusiveness of their rhymes.

If this chapter had attempted to summarize the history of dialect literature, I should have had to mention the Piedmontese, the Genoese, who have the most difficult dialect in Italy (Dante said that if you took the letter "X" from their dialect the Genoese would become mutes), and the Sicilians, whose Meli is at times as pure as Theocritus. I might have left out the Basiles and Corteses, diffuse Neapolitans who flourished two centuries earlier than Porta and Belli. But I should at least have had to quote a few of the thousands of exquisite lines by unknown Neapolitans, which show how much the Neapolitan mind had remained Greek. Here are four written at the request of a tavern keeper about 1750.

> Ah, let us eat and let us drink, my friends,
> While yet there's oil in the lamp, my brother;
> Who knows where we shall meet when this world ends,
> Who knows if there are taverns in the other.

Could this not have been written by one of those Athenian poets whose names we know from Meleager? Yet how quickly, in the classic Italian, their Hellenic flavor would turn bookish.

In all the dialects of Italy there are endless riches; in some, plebeian dash; in others, naïveté and fantasy; in all, delicacy alternating with violence and irony. But as I warned in my Preface, I wish to limit what I write here to what I know by personal experience. Besides, I do not know what books I could have used. Probably I should have found in Benedetto Croce the most original remarks about our dialect literature. In most intellectual matters, Croce is the man. Those who wish to know more always have the twenty volumes of Croce.

Certain foreign writers—who know so many details of Italian life and so little about the soul of Italy—have drawn hasty generalizations from the vitality of our dialects. Our feeling of unity is more artificial than real, they have decided. Actually, the history of our dialects, properly understood, proves the opposite. Our dialects produced poets when the classic language froze into stiffnecked artificiality—that is, when the country was deprived of its intellectual and political liberty. With the arrival of the *Risorgimento* and its great writers, the dialects lapsed into silence; they no longer filled a need.

It was only after decades of liberty that the dialects again demonstrated how alive and useful they were. Testoni in Bologna, Pascarella and Trilussa in Rome, Di Giacomo in Naples, have at times given us perfect works of art. Between 1900 and 1914 some of our most creative and popular novelists began going to the dialects to enrich their language. They also began to use vernacular dialogue. Fozzagaro makes several characters of his *Piccolo mondo antico* speak Venetian; Verga's peasants in *Cavalleria rusticana,* given world-wide popularity by Mascagni, use Sicilian; Matilde Serao has often made her petty clerks and her puppets *à la* Maupassant speak Neapolitan.

And yet this came when the Italian tongue had never been so full and rich. The old quarrel over the nature and the laws of language had died out. What Manzoni had never succeeded in establishing as a rule, free Italy instinctively adopted. There were no more purists to insist on classic rules or "Tuscan usage," for the Italian language —with or without "Tuscan usage"—had at last conquered the Italians.

The dialects enrich not only the literature but also the language of everyday conversation. They help to keep us alive. True Italian has no stereotyped phrases. Its words move about freely, with constant freshness of expression— a freshness which is beginning to disappear from the vocabulary of the ordinary educated Frenchman with its set, conventional phrases. But what foreigner, even among those who know Italy well, is capable of grasping these charming everyday individualisms in which one feels the pulsing soul of Italy?

In Italy the dialects themselves repeat the age-old law of the country—unity with Rome in essentials, diversity in every province in all besides.

CHAPTER VI

The Italians and Their Roots in the Soil

IT IS POSSIBLE for peoples to change their essential characteristics. The pleasure loving Briton of "Merrie England" disappeared beneath smug Victorian prudery. Even the body changes. A century of enthusiastic gymnastics has made grenadiers of the little Swedes of former times.

But it is certain that the stamp of the native earth is never erased. This is no matter of "Golden Centuries" or great revolutions or great men like Bismarck and Napoleon. A tradition of common joys and sorrows may have some part in forming local characteristics. But the great, though intangible, factor is the pattern of habits, the way of life, the mass of memories which have become flesh and blood.

A king of Hungary once affirmed that a nation which speaks only one language is imbecilic. If this is true— and within certain limits it certainly is true—the Italians are the luckiest people in Europe. An Italian is much richer for being at once Italian and Piedmontese, or Italian and Sicilian, than a Briton is to be English and Scottish, or English and Welsh. His region gives the Italian an older and more varied heritage than the Britisher derives from his Welsh poetic instinct or his realistic Scottish mysticism.

Every Italian is profoundly Italian, through the common

heritage of thought and language. But down deep he is still
more a Lombard, a Venetian, or a Neapolitan, although he
does not cease to belong to the common fatherland. There
is a real reason for the sort of unpleasant embarrassment
Italians experience whenever they meet a compatriot whose
accent reveals no contact with some particular province;
he sounds to them like an actor or a radio broadcaster. We
prefer even the accent of a Levantine; at least we can tell
whether he comes from Pera and Galata or from Alexan-
dria and Cairo. This explains the small attraction which
theatergoing—except to the patois theater—holds for most
Italians.

The same is true of books. The author who has visible
connections with the land has more chance of survival than
if he turns out only a literary Milan or a political Rome.
Manzoni would not be Manzoni if one did not feel the
Milanese in him. If Giusti is still so alive, it is because he
is as Tuscan as he can be. Even a universal mind like Benedetto Croce happily reveals his provincial, Neapolitan
character.

And what persistence there is in the provincial essence,
even when one has long been detached from it! I have
spent much time with the elderly Verga, my colleague in
the Senate. For thirty years he had been living in Milan,
and like many Sicilians he was cold and reserved. But a
youthful enthusiasm lighted his face when he felt that the
person talking to him was sincerely interested in Sicily.

Borgese has lived only at Milan—and, since fascism,
in the United States, where he is a professor at the University of Chicago. Yet the most perfect of the pages of his
novel *Rubè* are inspired by visions of his native Sicily.

Only one great Italian poet has escaped the mark of the

native earth—Leopardi. But he is the poet of despair.
D'Annunzio also escaped it. The influence of a few great
poets, like Baudelaire and Claudel and Whitman and
Tolstoy, has been deeper in him than the influence of his
native Abruzzi. Hence his sudden, world-wide vogue. But
this will also be the reason for the fate which awaits him
toward the year 2000—the fate of Chiabrera, Achillini,
Frugoni, and their like. They were famous in their life-
times, but today we cannot abide their artificiality and
bombast.

The theorists of fascism were suspicious of local traditions. They preferred centralization, alleging that it made
for strength. If they were sincere in this, they must have
had very little faith in the profound unity of Italy. In truth,
hidden behind their talk of unity, in every country, lurk
the police. If Bonaparte's phrases repeated the republican
slogan "United, indivisible France," when he was busy
destroying the old French provinces, it was only because
he wanted his informers everywhere, spying out the mur-
murers, while everywhere his bureaucratic machinery, with
its center in Paris, was facilitating the harvest of cannon
fodder for his sterile wars.

But even without the Corsican, France would have enjoyed great cultural unity. For centuries she had had marvelous Romanesque churches in the north as well as in
southern Moissac and Carcassonne; such things united the
whole country in worship of the same beauty. In Italy the
monuments themselves show a gradual change of conception and taste: while the ogive became the dominant type
in the north and the center of Italy, the Milan cathedral is
not reproduced even at nearby Piacenza, where the architecture becomes more squatty and massive. Going south,

the type changes constantly, from Genoa to Sarzane, from Lucca to Florence, from Florence to Siena. At Orvieto the idea is transformed; the presence of neighboring Rome has overshadowed the ogive and ousted it.

On the other side of the boot, on the Adriatic, Ravenna has kept the perfection of Byzantine art. No writer from abroad fails to discover that the aesthetic origins of Venice are in Ravenna. For the Frenchman Barrès the Orient begins at the Riva degli Schiavoni. The truth is that, like the other provinces of Italy, Venice has derived its art style from its own soil, if we may use that word here. If Venetian architecture is unique, it is because the architecture is conceived for a situation where the foundations rest on swampy ground and call for lightness and fluidity.

Marco Polo, who saw all there was to see of the Europe and Asia of his time, said that Venice could be compared to the only Chinese city of Fu-Kien whose streets are canals. Romaic Europe never reminded him of Venice. Trieste is the place which is really reminiscent of the Near East, just as the streets of Marseilles, around the Vieux-Port, recall Galata and Pera.

Every country has its Deep South. Liége is more of a southern city than Lyon; Marseilles and Toulon, which are as much on the Riviera as Genoa and Savona, are as southern in character as Athens—their whole character is more Greek than Latin. Genoa and maritime Provence, on the other hand, have nothing in common but their kitchen smells; the character of Provence is more Greek than Latin. Even the Venetian is infinitely more of a southerner than the Genoese, who, silent and withdrawn, seems to belong to the north of Europe.

The people of Genoa are more stubborn than the Scots and shrewder than the Jews—an Italian proverb says that it takes three Jews to make a Genoese. They are as clever in ocean trade as they are in their *scagni,* the airless little rooms from which they direct business operations totaling hundreds of millions. But they go home to palaces, hung with too many Van Dykes, which line one of the most gorgeous streets in the world. Here instead of cultivated conversation they have a sort of humor—half plebeian, half surly—and sometimes more vitriolic than one can find anywhere else in the world. It is one of the mysteries of Italy that this somber, harsh race produced the purest souls of the *Risorgimento,* like Mazzini and his tender, heroic mother Maria, and angelic Goffredo Mameli, whom one of Oudinot's bullets killed in Rome in 1849, after the young poet had written his famous hymn:

> Brothers of Italy,
> Italy has awaked.

This song still vibrates in our souls like an eternal fanfare of youth. The most intimate friends of young Mazzini were the brothers Ruffini, one of whom killed himself in prison rather than reveal the names of his accomplices in the struggle for liberty; they were Genoese also. And so was Christopher Columbus, whose life was a romance of restless energy.

The difference between Genoa and Tuscany is so great that it is hard to think of them as immediate neighbors. Actually they are not completely neighbors; the Lunigiana, which though small has a regional character of its own, cuts between.

The people of the Lunigiana—the province which

touches the sea at Spezia and the mouth of the Magra and whose steep mountains are studded by tiny hamlets—are descendants of the Apuans, whom the Romans enchained after long struggle and deported to Samnium. Some of the Apuans must have escaped deportation. My childhood was full of stories of revolt against the Austrian archduke who governed Modena and the Lunigiana. The dialect of the Lunigiana valleys is a mixture of Ligurian and Lombard, a violent speech, fit for these quarrymen who tear the marble from the bowels of the Apuan Alps.

Beyond the little cities of Sarzane, Massa, and Carrara are the first Tuscan town, Pietrasanta, and, an hour further on, Pisa; the traveler cannot miss feeling the difference. How strong the mysterious Etruscans must have been! The Tuscans of today have no link with other regions. The Florentine, when he has put on weight, looks like the *obesus Etruscus* of the old Etruscan vases. Like the Parisian who feels lost at Avignon or Orleans, the Tuscan is out of place in Milan, Naples, or even Rome. Other Italians admire his keen argument and lance-like irony, but they can never quite like him. Courteous, reflective, ironical, incapable of enthusiasm, sharpened by long experience in refined living, he is taken from time to time by accesses of that cold cruelty which Livy noticed in the Etruscans. The friends of the *francesi*, at the end of the eighteenth century, were ferociously assaulted only in Tuscany. Two hundred years later, in the disorders following the first World War, Tuscany was still the trouble center.

But the Florence of the past has been, next after Athens, the happy homeland of intelligence. This can still be discerned in its streets and *piazze*, despite a certain sterility now evident in younger Florentines.

The break is equally sharp between the other provinces. The eighteenth was the most cosmopolitan of centuries. From Catherine the Great to Tanucci of Naples, all cultivated minds thought in the same way, just as all sensitive spirits spoke the same language. Never were European frontiers less in evidence. And yet the enormous difference between the two greatest adventurers of the time, Casanova and Cagliostro, results from the difference of their native regions: Casanova, the Venetian, incarnates ardent love of life, sometimes to the point of vulgarity; while the Sicilian Cagliostro has the silent, uneasy violence of his island, where people are nordic and oriental at once, and where one can be more taciturn than a Scot, and always proud and sad. Right at hand, in Naples, people are—or seem to be—so very gay and frivolous.

The Italian language itself is only superficially the same in the mouths of various cultivated Italians. Of course, its salient features are essentially alike from the Alps to Sicily—for example, the absence of certain words like "château." A word for the English "manor" or the German "Hof" is not needed in Italy, because when the language developed the nobles had already been forced to join the commons within the city walls. In another sphere, one cannot fail to be delighted by the lovely vitality which certain words have preserved. "Gentile" is still as resonant today as it was in the immortal "latin sangue gentile," and "vago," which in French has come to mean only "undefinable," means in Italian today, as it meant to Dante, "charming" and "beautiful." "Leggiadro" and "leggiadria" are words which have become untranslatable into French or English, and yet fifty million Italians still know their meanings as they did when Agnolo Firenzuola defined them, in 1548, in his treatise, *Of the Beauty of Women*.

But what foreigner can grasp, even after years in Italy, the hundred shadings imparted to the most disciplined speech as well as the most commonplace by the little monosyllable exclamations—mildly approving "già," skeptically dubious "ma," tired and resigned "che vuoi"? All these have one special overtone at Milan, another at Naples, still another at Florence, where for instance the word "pazienza," heard a thousand times a day, attests the historic wisdom of a people which has behind it the old, old civilization of the Etruscans. We hear it everywhere, in village and city, each time disillusion blankets someone's hopes, when a storm destroys a contadino's crop or a tempest keeps a fisherman ashore or an artisan loses an order. A Christian moralist could maintain that the constant daily use of this word by every Tuscan proves that the Christian virtues are in the flesh and blood of the people. But wait; the same good chap whose favorite interjection is "pazienza" comes out, simply to reinforce what he is saying, with a blasphemy against the Virgin and the Saints which would bring a blush to the cheek of a grenadier.

The attitude of the Italian toward the surrounding countryside and his native soil can also be understood only as a very ancient heritage. The georgic accents of the Latin poets come to new life with Petrarch, with the *Ninfale fiesolano* of Boccaccio, in the verses of Poliziano and the *Epistles* of Ariosto, and even in the morbid sweetness of the *Pastor fido* of Guarini. Only yesterday this feeling for nature dictated Carducci's purest verses and made a poet of Pascoli, and of others whom fate has not made famous —Della Porta, Roccatagliata.

How does it happen that German writers—since Humboldt to be sure—have learnedly affirmed that Latins in general and Italians in particular lack a feeling for nature?

It is not entirely a case of smug German assurance that the true taste for nature does not exist outside Germany. Rather, these learned worthies have in naïve sincerity committed the error of identifying the sense of nature, so variable from civilization to civilization, with the form it takes among Germans. They did not happen to think that in Italy —which has been cut up and squared off by farm walls for thousands of years—poetry and love of the earth have developed under different aspects from those which touch peoples habituated to endless forests.

The German is still, with respect to nature, the direct heir of the Germanic tribesmen. He experiences the intoxication of solitude in the depths of the mysterious, noiseless forests. The trees, peaks, and rivers awaken in him the nostalgias and instincts of his ancestors. It is probably from these places and these instinctive memories that *Sturm und Drang* drew the sincerest expressions of its romanticism, so touching when not used as an argument for invading and oppressing other peoples.

The Italians, on the other hand, come down from the "Italiae cultores primi aborigines" who had already transformed the banks of our lakes and of the Po at the time when the Greeks were still convinced that the amber they came to buy at the mouth of the great river was an Italian product, so completely was the German and Baltic world lost in the fogs of the unknown.

Three thousand years ago Italy revered in the worship

of Saturn an earth rich in wheat on the plains and in vines
on the hills. The traces of these distant times have disappeared, but many estates and domains still preserve the
memory of the era when so many Roman or adopted-
Roman families marked them out in their present form:
Isola-Balba, Balbiano, Corneliano, Villa-Pompejana.

The nostalgia still alive in German hearts can be only
feebly approximated by Italians, whose love of nature is
part of their three-thousand-year-old love of rural life. But
the Piedmontese looks at the hills covered with the vines
which will produce his *barolo* and the Tuscan looks on his
olive groves with feelings of conquest and domination and
love for the land which he has mastered. His feeling for nature is profound, but it is idyllic, the opposite of the Wag-
nerian *Wanderlust* which seizes a German when he looks at
the nature which he has never been able to dominate. The
contrast between the Italian park (which was called "park"
after the gardens of Versailles) and the marvelous, invio-
late, and inhuman forest of Germany is eternal.

But what can foreigners know about the Italian soul and
its relation to nature, when, supplied with documents from
the libraries, they devote to the Lombard or Tuscan countryside only the tour indicated by the asterisks in Bae-
decker? I am Italian; I passed all my childhood and youth
in the country. But I must admit that I understood the long
silences and fixed gaze of the Italian peasants for the first
time only when I remembered them in China, where also
the love of the land assumes an almost religious tenderness.
It is easy to become ecstatic about the crowds of Japanese
who swarm, almost as if on pilgrimage, to the valleys of

flowering cherry trees or, in summer, scramble with emotion up the shifting trails of Fujiyama. For that, like the exaltation of the Germans for what still remains unconquered in nature, cannot fail to stir the dullest imagination. But the Chinese discovers in his fields a beauty of which he never tires; he sets before the tablets of his ancestors bread from wheat that has ripened in the same rows his father cultivated; and on the rare occasions when he feels called to pray, he prefers the rustic image of some god sheltered under a poor shaky arch near his own fields to the gilded statues of the neighboring city.

This is what the Italian feels for the light oil of his olives and the white and red wines from his few square yards of vineyard. These are the rewards of his deep-rooted union with an earth which no longer holds any terror for him and with which he has contracted a sort of secret marriage. His silent, solemn love has none of the ecstasy of German romanticism; it does not isolate the individual; it is latent in the minds of all Italians. It is capable of inspiring familial and patriotic tenderness, not the anguish and nostalgia of uneasy souls dreaming of a return to the life of pure instinct.

Whereas infinite forests and tumultuous rivers inspire the northerner's disgust for too tangible frontiers, the Italian countryside has been linked for hundreds of years with the cycles of the farming seasons, changing from moon to moon. Even the remains of our popular poetry falls in with them. The last remnant of our mystery plays, performed in the public squares of Tuscan villages in spring, is called the *maggio* (maytime). These feelings, al-

ready more collective than individual and as profound
then as they are now, were in the mind of Horace when he
wrote *Inveni portum.*

Can it be that the discomfiture of the German mind
comes from its inability to find the *portum* which the Italians have made the ideal of their lives?

CHAPTER VII

Italians and the Family Bond

THE ONE genuine discovery made by the nazi and fascist dictators, the one which has aided them powerfully to reach and to hold power, is this: a lie is a lie so long as you tell it infrequently; it becomes indisputable truth if you repeat it a thousand times, in a thousand papers, for six months on end. This repetition brought even those hostile to fascism to believe naïvely that before the fascist dictatorship Italy's social and political disorders were most dangerous. For the Fascists, this discovery was golden. The more they degraded and calumnified Italy, the more they justified their violent dictatorship.

No one remembers any longer that a certain disorder and malaise were common all over Europe after the war of 1914–18; that when "the occupation of the factories" took place in Italy genuine revolt broke out here and there in France, where the operating class succeeded in keeping the matter relatively hushed up; and that there were more strikes in England than there were in Italy during the same period.

At the most critical moment during the Italian strikes the British ambassador, Sir George Buchanan, came to ask me about them. Buchanan had come to Rome from Petrograd and had seen the Russian revolution. His colleagues called him the "scalded cat." I was personally very fond of the old gentleman, who revealed in all frankness what an intolerable life Lloyd George led his English ambassadors, to whom he sent instructions contrary to those issued by Lord Curzon. I replied as casually as possible:

"Foreign ministers have to be optimists by definition, Sir George. I shall tell you nothing. Only, let us go out together, without the formality of our autos and chauffeurs, and you can see for yourself."

It was Saturday evening. We took a taxi down the via Giulia, the long old street between the Piazza Farnese and the Tiber which had been the center of elegance of sixteenth-century Rome. Its palaces are now converted into workers' flats, and the ground floors have become taverns whose signs, hoisted over the peak of the big double doors, often cover the arms of some forgotten cardinal. We walked along, free even from the shadowing of the policemen. I offered no explanation to Buchanan, but the atmosphere of the Saturday evening spoke for me. On the doorsill of each inn were tables loaded with liters of light, fizzy Frascati, but instead of the comrades howling over their glasses we almost always saw some proud-looking fellow holding a youngster on his knees, with his wife beside him and two or three children already sampling their glass of *biondo asciutto*.

"Yes, you are right," said Buchanan, "a nation whose family life is so vital to everyone is held together by bonds stronger than the palaver about political doctrines."

Some months later, at an international conference, Lloyd George told me the story of Buchanan's walk, not without adding that Latin diplomats would never have been capable of such simple but "illuminating" observations as those of the British ambassador.

To know what home and family·mean to Italians, read the long series of letters from soldiers who died in the war, published between 1930 and 1933 in Benedetto Croce's *Critica* with a sober commentary by A. Omodeo. With admirably pure simplicity the sons call upon their mothers to sacrifice them not only because of patriotic duty but also in order that after the horror of the conflict the whole world may know true peace. This is in thousands of letters. The sentiment is mystical and religious, the only kind of sentiment which the sons thought worthy of the mothers.

Family sentiment, the earnest desire that their elders, wives, and children should be protected from hunger, was common and constant among millions of peasant soldiers who faced the Austro-German armies in the Alps from 1915 to 1918. In 1917, when our resistance weakened— as it weakened also among the English and the French, who were clever enough to talk a great deal less about their reverses—the new commander-in-chief, Diaz, revived morale by organizing aid for soldiers' families. His old-fashioned predecessor, Cadorna, would have worked wonders in the days when soldiers were driven with the lash. He never got the idea that the four million Italians under arms were citizens and frequently the heads of families. Diaz gained their confidence immediately by decreeing prompt and considerable death benefits. The government decreed other assistance measures, and the combatants, who knew how much their wives and children were suffering, especially in the South, were happy.

The mother is the most pathetic figure of the Italian family. In France she is powerful; she manages her house and her husband and children. In Italy she has no other authority than that she wins each day in the hearts of her sons. She establishes her place, or insinuates herself, only by her sweetness; she has only what she gives, what she is always ready to give.

Love of the home is mixed with love for the mother. The home is loved, in Italy, not for itself, but as a symbol of the continuity of the family. Even the most modest peasant hovel is an island among many other islands. Only at family feasts—births or marriages—does one lower the bridge between house and house and then only briefly. Yet this implies nothing like oriental seclusion. The Italians, like the ancient Greeks, feel that they were born for the market place; they are not eaten by the desire for solitude which often besets the Briton or the Scot. Thousands of years of city life together have taught every Italian the art of remaining alone in the midst of the noisy crowd; alone —of course, in the Italian sense of the word—with his wife and children. This is, by the way, the source of the Italian art of living together in harmony, three or four sons under the same roof in farm or palace.

Among Italians of old families affection is infinitely greater for the villa—whether an old, patched-up farm or an architectural marvel *à la* Palladio—than for the palace in town. The villa has nothing in common either with the French "château" or the English "cottage." Even when it looks like a formidable, towered castle, it is never more than a villa. In Italy the château of Versailles would be the villa of Versailles. The Italian of an old family does not feel that he loses caste if he sells his palace in Milan, Piacenza, or Genoa to a bank; but he considers himself a traitor to his name if he sells, except in greatest extremity, the oldest of his villas, where in ancient closets have been kept the costumes of the eighteenth century, whose library holds a copy of the French *Encyclopédie* which an ancestor got from Paris during the Enlightenment, and the marvelous quartos of the Italian classics printed by Bodoni two generations later—the villa that a Baedecker-bearing tourist would sometimes judge from its exterior to be a graceless old building, whereas its hidden gardens have fountains worthy of Bernini, and the walls of its living rooms are hung with Flemish and Italian canvases of the *sicconto;* the villa whose proprietors, for ten leagues around, are called, not by vain titles like "marquis" and "count," but simply, and with an affectionate respect which excludes all servility, "Signor Cesare," "Signor Carlo," "Signor Ascanio." For (and this is something foreigners often do not know) there are whole regions in Italy where, at most, titles are used on the envelopes of letters, never in conversation, even when an "inferior" addresses a "superior." To such an extent is the life of Italy, as history has made her, that of a genuine democracy, in spite of—when not outside—all the laws of her administrations.

CHAPTER VIII

The Italians and Their Religion

OUTSIDE Italy the belief is common that Italians have little religious ardor and certainly no mystical tendencies. Yet few European peoples have been so moved by waves of religious sentiment as we have.

A generation before Saint Francis, Joachim of Floris revived the souls of half of Italy. Dante puts him in Paradise: "The Calabrian Father Joachim, endowed with prophetic mind." And he is venerated even today in the churches of Calabria, where on his feast they still sing the Latin antiphon which either suggests or echoes Dante's line: "Beatus Joachim, spirito dotatus prophetico, dixit futura et praesentia."

Like Saint Francis, Joachim was the son of rich parents. And like the Little Poor Man he gave away his wealth. After a foot pilgrimage to Jerusalem he took refuge in Calabria with the Cistercians of Sambucina as a simple lay brother. Here, however, the parallel with Saint Francis ends. He devoted many years to the study of the Bible, composing works in which, with a foretaste of the rumblings of Savonarola, he saw as the salvation of the Church the transfer of the pastoral function into the hands of the monks and contemplatives. The condemnation of the Holy See as a temporal power seemed implicit in his work, but he was not prideful, and he inclined before the verdict of the pope and the bishops. This saved him. In 1212 the Lateran Council condemned this pure ascetic; but subsequently the Church protected him and finally beatified him.

The heresies and deep hatreds which divided Europe in his time prospered less in Italy than elsewhere. Joachim preached a Christianity which forsook the coldness of the letter to rise to the purity of the evangelic spirit, and for the Italians this sufficed. What heretical movements appear to have spread during the thirteenth century did so especially because they were inspired and encouraged by the Emperor Frederick II in his struggle against the popes.

Joachim of Floris was not long dead when his heritage, stripped of its apocalyptic elements, was gathered up by the Umbrian Francis of Assisi. Francis entrusted the salvation of Christianity to the inner man and the salvation of the Church to the effort of souls, to the unanimous aspiration of the faithful. One can dare say that this is the first human message to approach the message of Christ.

The whole of Saint Francis is in his *Hymn to Our Brother the Sun,* the true, thirteenth-century title of which was *Laudes creaturarum,* the most inspired of all religious poetry except the *Te Deum:*

Most high, omnipotent, good Lord,
Praise, glory, benediction all are Thine.
To Thee alone do they belong, most High,
And there is no man fit to mention Thee.

Praise be to Thee, my Lord, with all Thy creatures,
Especially to my worshipful brother sun,
The which lights up the day, and through him thou dost brightness
　　give;
And beautiful is he and radiant with splendor great;
Of Thee, most High, signification gives.

Praised be my Lord, for sister moon and for the stars,
In heaven Thou hast formed them clear and precious and fair.

Praised be my Lord for brother wind
And for the air and clouds and fair and every kind of weather,
By the which Thou givest Thy creatures nourishment.
Praised be my Lord for sister water,
The which is greatly helpful and humble and precious and pure.

Praised be my Lord for brother fire,
By the which Thou lightest up the dark,
And fair is he and gay and mighty and strong.

Praised be my Lord for our sister, mother earth,
Which sustains and keeps us
And brings forth diverse fruits with grass and flowers bright.

Praised be my Lord for those who by Thy love forgive
And weakness bear and tribulation.
Blessed those who shall in peace endure,
For by Thee, most High, shall they be crowned.

Praised be my Lord for our sister, the bodily death,
From the which no living man can flee.
Woe to them who die in mortal sin;
Blessed those who shall find themselves in Thy most holy will,
For the second death shall do them no ill.

Praise ye and bless ye the Lord, and give Him thanks,
And be subject unto Him with great humility.[1]

No one can fail to see that, unlike so many in his time,
Saint Francis has less fear of a vengeful God than trust
in a God of love and pity. Although they could not reach
his lyric heights, his disciples did not cease believing that
this lowly world is something more than a vale of tears.
Had not Francis stipulated in his Rule: "Let the brothers
be happy in the Lord, and joyful"? Yet these simple men,
these joyful ones, often turned out to have the souls of

---

[1] *The Writings of St. Francis of Assisi,* translated by Father Paschal Robinson, Philadelphia, Dolphin Press, 1906, p. 152.

martyrs, especially in the troubled generation which followed that of Saint Francis.

An anonymous document of the late fourteenth century relates the torture, at Florence, of one of the Little Brothers, also anonymous, one of those Franciscans who were determined to follow the strictest rule of the *Poverello*. This almost unknown text is worth reproducing. I know few documents in which the Italy of the poor, with its despair and its hopes, is described with greater freshness or more permanent truth. How many times these pages have come back to my mind when, in the humble villages of Lombardy and Liguria under full sway of the Fascists I have witnessed the heroic resistance of two or three against hundreds of drunken, raging Facists—resistance which at times became a sort of religious sacrifice, the like of which I doubt was seen in Germany during the Nazi conquest.

Here is the story of the death of the unknown monk as it is written in the pure, stark language of the time of Dante.

As soon as Friar Michael appeared on the threshold of the prison, alone, half-naked, reciting verses of the Gospels, the people cried together:

"Oh, why do you want to die?"

And he: "I want to die for Christ."

"But you do not die for Christ."

And he again: "For the truth!"

Someone added: "You do not believe in God!"

He replied: "I believe in God and in the Virgin and in Holy Church."

And others: "Wretch, you are possessed of the Devil."

"God keep me from it."

But his replies were rare; he made them only when it seemed to him necessary; and rarely he lifted his eyes to the people.

When he had come to the corner of the *Proconsolo,* where there was a great noise of people, some of the faithful approached him and murmured:

"Friar Michael, say a prayer to God for us."

Then, lifting his eyes, he replied: "Go! And God's blessing with you, Catholic Christians."

Further on, by the base of Santa Liberata, someone cried to him: "Fool that you are, believe in the pope."

And he, lifting his head again: "You have made a God of this pope; you shall see what straits these popes will put you in."

And later, to the same people: "These *paperi* (pun on the words *papa* [pope] and *papero* [duck]) have left you in a pretty puddle."

The crowd, wondering, observed: "He goes to death with joy."

Having come to San Giovanni, as they cried to him "Repent, repent," he replied: "I do repent all my sins."

Beyond the bishops' palace, someone cried: "You call on no one to pray for you."

And he, in a loud voice: "I beg all Catholic Christians to pray to God for me."

Between the Mercato Vecchio and Calimala someone called: "Live, live!"

And he, "You should be afraid of living in Hell."

At the New Market they said to him again: "Repent, repent."

He replied: "Repent your own sins, and your usury, and your false dealings."

And at the Square of the Priors someone else: "Repent your error; save your life."

And he: "Before all else, the Catholic faith, the truth."

One man who followed at more than a bow-shot's distance among the others cried out to him: "You are a devil's martyr. You think that you know more than all the masters. Do you think that Master Luca, the theologian, would risk losing his soul if he knew you were telling the truth? Does he not know more than you?"

"If I remember rightly, Master Luca knows very well that he possesses a great deal of money, against the rule of his order, and he clings to it."

The same man cried again: "You claim that we are neither Christians nor baptized."

And he, looking the other in the eye: "Not at all; I say that you are Christians and baptized, but that you do not behave like Christians."

Again the same man: "Voice of the people, voice of God. . . ."

And Michael answered: "The voice of the people put Jesus on the Cross and sent Peter to death."

Other quarters began to attack him still more: "He is possessed; he is a heretic," they cried.

And he: "I am not a heretic; I shall never be one."

One of his faithful called to him by name, urging him to think on the Passion of Jesus. Then with happy face, he turned toward this man and replied: "Faithful Catholic Christians, pray God that he give me strength. . . ."

When he arrived at Santa Croce, near the Portal of the Brothers, these latter showed him the portrait of Saint Francis. He raised his eyes to heaven and exclaimed: "Saint Francis, my father, pray for me!"

Then he spoke to the Franciscans who were on the steps and cried to them in a loud voice: "The Rule of Saint Francis, your Rule, has been condemned. You send to death those who are determined to keep it."

He repeated these words several times. A number of the monks shrugged, the others lowered their hoods over their faces.

Someone cried to him: "It is you who will to die."

"I do not will to die. It is they who kill me."

"But they do so because you will it."

"Rather than deny the truth."

"But even Saint Peter denied."

And then others added: "In your place, Saint Peter would repeat the denial."

"He would not. If he did he would be doing wrong."

Some of the faithful having reproached those who urged him to recant, the archers noticed it and cried: "He has disciples here."

Several of these slunk away, but a woman began to shout: "Stay strong, martyr of Christ! Soon you shall receive the crown of the saints."

I do not know what he replied, for a great noise went up.

When he came to the pile they began to make a lot of smoke, to frighten him. While this was happening a young man arrived, sent by the Ten to set him free if he should recant.

Seeing Michael's determination, one of the officers exclaimed: "The devil must be in him."

"Or Christ, perhaps," said the young man.

Michael fell on the pile, his face turned up toward heaven. Many sighed, even among those who had been against him: "He seems like a Saint."

On Saturday morning, the faithful having taken away his body, the preaching fathers expostulated regretfully from their pulpits: "There should have been guards posted where they buried him. You will see. He will be canonized and made a saint."

Nowhere else in literature is there such a gathering of Italian types: pure souls and cowards; hypocrites and bullies.

After the Council of Trent the forms of our religious fervor changed. Saint Philip Neri was perhaps the last of the great Italian saints to possess the joyous intoxication of Francis of Assisi. After him there began a series of ascetics like Saint Louis Gonzaga.

For centuries now, one of our constant political preoccupations has been the search for a balance of power between State (which at the time of the Guelphs and the Ghibellines was called the Emperor) and the Church. This involves the most highly developed exercise of what I shall discuss later as the very Italian spirit of compromise.

Even the most ardent Ghibellines have never freed themselves of a certain attachment to the Roman Church.

Everyone has recognized it as a masterpiece of Italian organization. True, the city of Rome never missed an occasion to undermine the temporal power of the popes, at least up to the beginning of the sixteenth century. Italian tale tellers have often described with exquisite pleasure the outrages inflicted on pontiffs who were too avid of temporal success. But never did the Italians take the side of the anti-popes; for us, these were only puppets in the hands of the German emperors. Not only were they of foreign manufacture but even for Italians outside the Catholic faith they would have upset the balance and germanized Italy.

On her side, the Church in Italy has never been stiff-necked. She has never attempted to hinder the spread of Italian masterpieces like the *Divine Comedy* and the *Canzoniere* of Petrarch, although here and there they treat her harshly. If she did proscribe a work of Dante, *De monarchia*, it was because the work was in Latin and read by no one. She was tolerant also of Ariosto, whose satires and comedies scarcely spared either the clergy or the traffic in indulgences, which was an open sore during the first part of the sixteenth century.

This tradition of tolerance did not die in the Counter Reformation. In 1617, and again in 1667, the Spanish Inquisition solemnly put Dante and Petrarch on its Index. Rome was also asked to take action, but the popes suddenly went deaf and even ridiculed the Spanish bigots. The popes were Italians and knew these poets by heart. Dante and Petrarch were part of their intellectual lives. How could they ban them?

If medieval and reformation heresies took so little hold on Italy, this was because spiritual liberty—especially in the earlier period—was more freely enjoyed in Italy than in any other European country. The *pataria* of the Lombards and the *catari*, coming from the Orient, gained foothold in Italy only as social revolts. They were the Italian form of the French *Jacqueries*.

Foreigners—especially those from Catholic countries—have in the past found it difficult to understand how complex and subtle the political relations between the Italian people and the Church really were. They should never forget that Dante, the world's greatest Catholic poet, did not hesitate to put several popes among the simonists in the third circle of Hell. In an apostrophe that for five hundred years Italians have known by heart, the poet, in spite of his reverence for the Holy Keys, cries out:

> Silver and gold ye make your God; and how
> Differ ye from the idolater, except
> That he to one, ye to a hundred bow?
> Ah, Constantine, mother of how much woe
> Was, not thine own conversion, but that dower [2]
> Which on the first rich father didst bestow. [3]

The movement which appeared to too many foreign Catholics as the Italian "anti-clericalism" of the *Risorgimento* and the nineteenth century was only a tradition of anti-temporalism which went back to Christendom's greatest poet, Dante himself. Luigi Sturzo, a holy priest and pro-

---

[2] Rome, which according to a tradition accepted by all in Dante's time, Constantine was supposed to have presented to Sylvester I. It was only a century after Dante that Valla proved the absence of all historic truth from this legend.

[3] *The Divine Comedy of Dante Alighieri*, translated by J. B. Fletcher, New York, Macmillan, 1931, "The Inferno," XIX, ll. 112–17.

found scholar, has thought it his duty as an Italian and a Catholic to demonstrate this on several occasions.[4]

Let me cite, finally, an episode from the life of Manzoni, the Italian poet whose *Inni sacri* are the highest and purest Catholic lyrics of the nineteenth century. He was very old, and lived in Milan, going rarely to Turin for the meetings of the Senate, of which he had been a member since the constitution of the Kingdom, in 1860. His intimates advised him to spare his health, rather than make the trip to the temporary capital to vote, as he said he wanted to do, on the law making Rome the capital of Italy. But the old man replied: "How shall I dare present myself before God, as I shortly must, if I have neglected to do the Church the greatest service that could possibly be done for her, the suppression of the temporal power?" Six hundred years after Dante, the same words—and once more from the lips of a great Catholic.

Pius XI, whose admiration for Manzoni was unlimited, often used to quote Manzoni's verses or passages from *The Betrothed* in his encyclicals and addresses. During the first months of his pontificate he gave an audience to my father, who had been his close friend when as Monsignor Ratti the pope had been director of the Ambrosian Library at Milan. At the Vatican the conversation fell once more upon Manzoni. The pope exclaimed: "How happy I should be, my dear friend, if I could induce all Italian Catholics to read and read again all of Manzoni." This was the same pope who in 1931 published his encyclical *Non abbiamo bisogno* against the pagan theories of Italian fascism, while

---

[4] See, especially, his monumental work, *Church and State*, and also an article which he published in the New York Catholic review, the *Commonweal* (April, 1941), under the title, "Has the Italian Character Changed?"

so many foreign Catholics, victims of hypocritical propaganda, believed, or were trying to believe, that the fascist regime had reëstablished religious values.[5]

[5] The Jesuit, Father Oddone, wrote in 1941, in the *Civiltà Cattolica*, the famous review published by his society:

If in fascist Italy it is esteemed useful to appear religious, one can see people who are certainly not pious play the role of champions of religious orthodoxy and of the faith. . . . Against this spirit of hypocrisy and falsehood . . . which threatens to obscure and weaken, even among Catholics, respect for truth and the worship of truth, every man of good will, faithful to the Gospels, should react in the most vigorous manner possible.

The censors pretended not to see the attack. Such is their system where matters of philosophy are concerned, since such things are unlikely to penetrate to the masses. The fascist censorship is very aware that those who read reviews like the *Civiltà Cattolica* are not Fascists, even though—for opportunistic reasons—there are some who pretend to be.

CHAPTER IX

Italians of the North and Italians of the South

THE DIFFERENCE between the North and the South is no greater in Italy than in France or Germany or the United States, but in Italy the break between them is perhaps a bit sharper. This may be why the French, when they invaded Italy under Charles VIII, sang: "We shall conquer *all* the Italies." Yet a thousand times, when the train for the French Riviera pulled into Valence, an hour below Lyon, I have heard northern Frenchmen exclaim scornfully, "Now we are out of France."

Admitting that the cleavage is more noticeable in Italy, it is no less true that the difference is not one of race—of Greek influence in the South and of German and Celtic influence in the North. The explanation is historical. For whole centuries the States of the Church made a zone in the center of the peninsula which had nothing in common with the rest of the country, was neither northern or southern in character, and hindered all contact between the two sections.

During this time they seemed to be separated by an insuperable distance. One of the joys of Italians who read Dante is his habit of throwing in parenthetical verses which describe with matchless exactitude the views and landscapes of the peninsula. From the Lago Maggiore to Carrara and from Venice to Florence—he had been everywhere. But never a verse about the South; he had never seen it, and Dante described only what he had seen. Petrarch, Ariosto, Machiavelli, and Manzoni never went there either. In the fourteenth century, Boccaccio was a unique exception. In the nineteenth, Leopardi went only when he was sick and Mazzini stayed only because he was in prison.

The real substitution of a single Italy for the "two Italies" was the work of the railroads. One day Bonaparte got the idea—in one of his Rousseauistic reveries—that the Creator would have done better to join Calabria, Sicily, and Sardinia with Latium, thereby rounding out an Italy which was inconveniently long for the recruiting of cannon fodder. One of the principal merits of the liberal Italian governments between 1860 and 1890 is that they did "round out" Italy, by creating, in spite of financial difficulties which were often staggering, a great system of rapid communications right down to the heel and toe of the boot. They did it in spite of mountains and torrents and precipices which constituted the toughest engineering problem in Europe. In actual fact the South Italian railroads possess twice as many bridges, trestles and tunnels as there are in any other European railway system. I was present in 1919 at an Italo-German railway conference when the chief of the Italian delegation spoke of the perfection of the German lines and the German chief replied: "Yes, ours are very fine, but now that I have seen the difficulties and the variations in grade of your Italian roads I wonder whether our staff would have been capable of the feats yours managed with a much smaller supply of rolling stock than we had."

The long period of separation from the rest of Europe is probably what makes the Italian South a land of philosophers. Giordano Bruno, Campanella, and Vico represent three aspects of the speculative audacity of yesterday's Italy, as Benedetto Croce is her living glory today. Among philosophers of the North of Italy during the first half of the nineteenth century, like Rosmini-Serbati and Gioberti, foreign influences are evident. In Croce even Hegel is only an aid in the elaboration of a new idea.

Those who, in Italy as elsewhere, are disgusted with the attitude of superiority which the North of every country displays toward the South, should be pleased to think that it is a Neapolitan, Croce, who gives all Italy—and perhaps all Europe—the example of a tireless struggle, conducted with austere serenity, for the ideal of human liberty, although every day in danger.[1]

While the Italian North has given the world some of its richest artists, not only in poetry, painting, and sculpture but even in music—Verdi was born on the plains of the Po —the South has produced our purest heroes of the spirit, audacious in thought and restrained in expression. They begin with the medieval doctors of the School of Salerno, who instituted the practice of braving the fury of the people so that they could search for the mystery of life in corpses stolen from the cemeteries.

As for the average Italian of the South, he is to the Italian-in-general what the latter is to the Europeans of the North, with the same accentuation of qualities and defects. And there is a similar analogy in the inevitability of legends and ready-made formulae which attempt to explain this accentuation. Even among the Italians of the North,

---

[1] October, 1926, my library was sacked by Fascists in Naples, and in the same night a country house of mine in the North, at Forte dei Marini, was burned by other Fascists—in both cases by orders from "above."

the old portrait of the lazy, verbose southerner continues in circulation.

To the person who has seen enough of Naples when he has visited the museum, Capri, Pompeii, and Vesuvius, the well-dressed but underfed petty bourgeois who strolls at Chiaia and on the via Toledo does indeed seem to be taking nonchalantly an endless and aimless constitutional. And, to our great astonishment, he seems to like music less than the northerner and to prefer the facile melodies of the Piedigrotta, the symbol, for foreigners, of the Neapolitan's delight in life. How many northern Italians have ever penetrated the darkness of Piedigrotta—it is always night at Piedigrotta—and have even suspected that the joys to be found there were in the hearts of drunken Germans and hysterical Polish women, while the sad Neapolitan masses, hidden by the night, had thrown off the braggart smile of the via Toledo to weep for a life whose mediocrity was rendered ever more cruel by the unreality of their pathetic dreams?

The factitious portrait of the gay and shiftless southerner is getting out of style. Fact has been stronger than prejudice. It is enough to meet, at Milan or Turin, merchants or technicians of the Puglie or of the Basilicata. Distant, silent, obstinate—they are the very opposite of the old cliché. There are indeed specific cases of unsuccessful southerners, especially among the children of a poor, inert bourgeoisie, who dream of becoming minor government clerks. They produce the strange paradox, that whereas fascism had more sincere partisans in the North than in the South, the majority of fascist police agents, officers, and hatchet-men is composed of southern petty bourgeois, happy with even a fascist uniform as long as it attaches them to a share of the taxpayers' money.

The struggle of the Lombards against the swamps of the vast plains of the Po lasted four or five centuries, but in the end they triumphed, and made their earth one of the richest regions of Europe. In the South the task is more heroic, for it has constantly to be renewed. Except in two or three oases, such as the Campagna, the land is like the slopes of Vesuvius on which, tirelessly, new vines are planted after each eruption of the volcano. The southern Italian's struggle with his land is one of the rarest examples of human resistance, but the struggle is silent, with no grand gestures. That is why people prefer the clichés which the northerners of every country cherish with respect to the South.

The Normans who took over Naples had proved in England that they were one of the most vigorous peoples of their time. But in southern Italy they were quickly swallowed up. The French and the Spanish later met a more or less similar fate. The study of historical realities shatters the cocksure theories that the Italian South inevitably differs from a North strongly tinctured with things germanic. At the very most the races, if in this case one may even speak of races, are like the rivers which suddenly disappear into the depths of a valley and after a long course below ground come back to the surface in the form of small lakes or springs.

The only true difference between the North and the South of Italy is economic. The land below Rome is infinitely poorer than that of the North. Just as the Greek civilization of Magna Graecia (Southern Italy) was ephemeral and probably less brilliant than we have thought, just so Rome was an inattentive stepmother to this scarcely known South, whence she heard vague rumors of agrarian revolt, this South where, before Rome, opulent Carthage recruited its mercenaries.

The southern Italians complain at times about the egoism of the industrial North. They should complain more especially about the poets, both their own and others. Seven centuries before Christ a Greek lyrist sang of Calabria as "the happiest of the world's countries." Poor, tragic Calabria, which will always be one of the most sterile lands of Europe! From Virgil to Goethe literature has created the legend of the happy southerner who scarcely deigns to rise and gather in the fruits of the earth growing lush about him.

Stranger yet is the fact that for a long time the southerners themselves believed this tale. Today it is as painful as it is comic to read over the solemn memorials that Naples sent to Victor Emmanuel in 1860, with their description of the treasures that the ancient realm of the Two Sicilies declared itself proud to place at the disposal of United Italy. In part this was an effect of the economic segregation in which the South had lived under the Bourbons; but it was especially the result of the artistic legend. How could a land of enchanting vistas like Naples, Sorrento, and Palermo, with a hundred places "where blows the orange tree," be a poor country? People had forgotten that behind those heavenly coasts the desert reigns, because where there is no water, sunlight is only a snare. Unlike the rest of the country, the South has rain only in winter. Instead of a Po, an Arno, and a Tiber, there are only torrents, dry in summer and rising to destructive fury during the winter. When you speak of the Italian South, you must never forget that drought destroys three crops out of ten with astronomical precision. The aqueduct of the Puglie, the gigantic construction projected and executed by the liberal governments of Italy (although fascist publicity has passed it off on the world as a product of its regime) has not afforded a complete solution of the problem. If the Italian North has anything to reproach itself for, it is of having been tardy to understand its duties and responsibilities toward the South.

Now that the liberal and democratic regimes are interrupted in Italy, it is the style to single out their faults. The truth is that they did much for the South, but that the problem was formidable. In the last days of his life, on the eve of unification, Cavour, who was never dubious of his own abilities, wrote: "Harmonizing the North with the South of the peninsula is even more difficult than to struggle against the Empire of Austria." When Italians feel irritated by certain summary and vain judgments which foreigners pass upon them, let them remember, if they are northerners, what their falsely sympathetic forefathers said of their brothers of the South; and let them beat their breasts.

CHAPTER X

Italy and Foreign Visitors and Writers

I SAID in the preceding chapter that the railroads were of powerful assistance in fusing the Italians of the North with those of the South after the long historical break caused by the establishment of the Pontifical State. But it was easy for Italians to rediscover each other; the obstacle between them, though old, was never anything but artificial. For foreigners, the opposite happened. The railroads—and later the auto—destroyed their chance of entering into real and deep contact with the living Italy, the Italy of souls, intellects, and ideas. After the railroads came, foreigners wrote books which were often very beautiful, on the Greek ruins in Calabria or on Milan and Venice, on Sicilian art or on the Uffizi of Florence. But there were no more Goethes or Brownings or Stendhals or Shelleys.

As a child I delighted in the old travel guides of eighteenth-century Italy; I have never forgotten the emotions with which I read a *Guida di viaggio per un gentilhuomo polacco* and its four-column appendix of *Conversazione in italiano, latino, francese e polacco.* In both the book and the *conversazione* was a bit of everything, mixed in a hodge-podge like life itself: archeology and cookery, museums and women, roads and social life. By comparison, the *Sensations d'Italie,* in which Paul Bourget swoons over the minor Sienese painters, is a cemetery for embalmed ideas. One has the feeling that authors of his type have never really lived in Italy. They are driven by their contracts with publishers to think of nothing but the beautiful pages that will grow out of their scribbled notes. Thus they miss that integration of the ancient with the modern which alone permits one to understand a living nation.

The Italian—especially the common Italian—is at once so complex and so simple that one can only smile at the strangers who think that in a year or so on the peninsula they have discovered the key to the Italian character. Paradox or not, it is easier to discover the complexity of Italians than their simplicity. How could the peasant or artisan who is such an infallible judge of the foreigner or the squire he is dealing with be anything but complex? Let the proprietor of a *podere* or of a villa, or the foreigner who has hired one for a time, beware. If the people round about make up their minds that he is *superbo* ("proud") or *prepotènte* ("arrogant"), he will never obtain anything from anyone—not even at thrice the money paid by foreigners and squires who have a reputation for pleasantness and cordiality.

To understand a foreign people, intelligence and education are worth little if they are not vivified by humane fellow feeling. When sometimes I dare to maintain that I understand the Chinese, the only subjective reason I can give is that when, after a twelve-year absence, I saw once more the bulging roofs of the Yungting-Men through the dusty atmosphere of Chi-li, my heart throbbed almost as if I were returning to my own country. And yet China has almost everything to offer—she was my tutor in relativity—except such sentimental emotions.

What makes the traveler is, not the distance he has come, but his capacity for seeing and for identifying himself with the soul of the country. I have seen standard-brand tourists in Mongolia and true travelers on the plains of Lombardy and in the villages of the Var. This capacity for understanding is not to be learned from books, but must be bought at the price of a part of our very existence. The French who, wanting to go further than the museums, arrive saturated with Stendhal, and the Germans who come to Italy with their Goethe in their hands, are like certain oriental converts to Catholicism who come to church and read from the prayerbook used by all the faithful; they do read it, but not with the same emotion.

Goethe himself saw only a fragment of Italy; he turned his back in distaste on the Middle Ages, out of scorn for Germany; as a pagan—or unwitting Protestant—his antipathy for what the Church has given Italy since the origin of the Communes was excessive. Stendhal loved Italy, indeed, the Italy of Dante as much as the Italy of the *settecento* and the Italy of the churches as much as that of the palaces and vineyards. But it is not so much that Stendhal's Italy is the true Italy as that Stendhal had an essentially Italian character. When Italians judge Stendhal, they must see things as they are, unless they are more interested in hearing themselves praised than in hearing realities—and realities are beautiful enough.

Another of the numerous manifestations of the moral poverty of the Fascists is that they anxiously seek praise, not for our art, but for our industries, which are magnificent and which had won their place in the world a half-century before fascism. Fascist publicity presents them as creations of its regime. The same naïve vanity was apparent four generations ago in Japan, when the Japanese of the first years of the Meiji era hid or destroyed their lacquer work and their porcelains to show Europeans how modern they had become. All this is more ridiculous than hateful; but if, even in the life of the spirit, one prefers realism to lyricism, it must not be forgotten that Stendhal's intense love for Italy was more than all else a reaction of disgust against get-rich-quick France. What we should cherish in Stendhal is that he felt keenly the extent to which the natural dignity of the commoner and the peasant makes the essential nobility of our people.

If Stendhal was conscious of the depth and the contrasts in souls, it is because he lived in Italy as a man, not as a writer, and—his adepts would add—as a solitary man. Barrès was wrong to make Stendhal a "professor of energy," if "energy" means success in life. He could have said it of Balzac, who was always in pursuit of social success. But Stendhal's energy was the energy of interior passion, not of exterior action. What he did always seemed to him worth doing only when not spoiled by the prospect of a recompense. This perhaps explains Stendhal's meager success with women. He envied the man who loved, but not the man of numerous feminine conquests. He would have been horrified by the Valmont of *Les Liaisons dangereuses*.

On the contrary, Byron and Chateaubriand, Lamartine and Ruskin, never went deep enough to find the spirit of Italy. For them Italy was only a pretext for the study of art. Stendhal's salvation was that he wrote for distant readers. The poor consul at Civitavecchia had the good luck to lack a publisher, whereas the others were harassed from London and Paris for *Odes* and *Memories from beyond the Tomb*.

The conclusion is a paradox only on the surface. The richer and more powerful the literature of a people and the more its artists have fixed its lineaments in miraculously famous canvases and statues, the more do foreign visitors see this people as if it had congealed beneath a mist of ancient and tiresome formulae, from which escape is impossible.

The *terribilità* of Dante is probably based on a whole series of psychological legends, just as a whole side of Stendhal's character cannot be explained if we forget his passionate love, almost the love of a collector, for fifteenth-century Italian chronicles. I have known Germans to maintain that the history of England is fuller of gore, violence, and treason than that of any other European nation. When they saw my astonishment, they referred me to the tragedies of Shakespeare about the Henries.

In conclusion, we Italians measure the understanding of a foreign writer or visitor by the judgment which he forms of our common people, whose roots are still firm in the soil. I do not mean by this that we want them to be praised only; the English novels of old Ouida, novels in which every *zampognaro* ("bagpiper") is a hero and every gondolier a poet, ring as false in our ears today—no matter how popular they were with our grandparents—as the Italophobiac idiocies of some Englishman or other who remembers of his trip to Italy only the bogus antique statuette someone sold him.

Would it not be better for foreigners either to resign

themselves to admit that the Italian people, beneath its unconcerned exterior, is a closed book to them, or else to settle down for ten years into an Italian countryside? Perhaps they could get nearer the truth if they simply looked about, watching the vineyard keepers on the hills of Rome, the shepherds of the Abruzzi mountains, the proprietors of half-acre farms in Liguria or Lunigiana. They could not help admiring their perfect equilibrium, a balance which even resists contact with the cities and the clumsiness of military life. Let them watch a regiment of infantry pass through the streets of an Italian city; in no other country will they get so complete an impression of watching thoroughbreds. Whoever has lived, as I have, beside these men in the relative freedom of the soldier's life, has retained an astonishing memory of their marvelous cleverness in making the best of their meager resources, their quickness of understanding even before orders arrive, and their terribly precise judgment of the personal qualities of their chiefs. Those tall, gay peasants from Lombardy, or the short, sad ones from the Puglie, with whom I spent so many days between 1915 and 1918 on the Eastern Front, seem to me the living illustration of a phrase of Palladio: "Man should have an eye to four things, air, water, earth, and self-mastery; the first three are things of nature, the fourth of power and of the will."

The fifty thousand Italians on the Macedonian front had the Serbs immediately at their right, and next the French, and then the English. All were fighting the same enemy, since the German, Austrian, Hungarian, and Bulgarian units had been intermingled by orders from Berlin. Writing after the year of grace 1941, when millions of Italians have died in Albania and Greece in combat—against Italy's permanent best interests—with the Greeks and our Serbian allies of 1915–18, let me recall how the instinctive brotherhood and sympathy between Italians and Serbs on the old Eastern Front was admired even by such veteran skeptics as Guillaumat and Franchet d'Esperey.[1] When, after the armistice of 1918, the latter came to Constantinople where, as Italian High Commissioner, I had preceded him, he spoke even then of the Italo-Jugoslav entente as he had seen it on the battlefield, an entente which contrasted so sharply with the cheap divide-and-rule politics, which I later overturned, of Baron Sonnino during his stay at the Consulta.

I replied to the French chief: "General, it is too bad that when you foreign personages come to Italy you meet only other personages; if you could get an idea of the longstanding good sense and simple generosity of the Italian common folk, you would respect them. I am counting on these basic qualities of the people to obliterate, in time, the vanities and prejudices which menace our future in the East."

What I said then about the Balkans and the Levant, I repeat today with reference to Europe, despite the follies and crimes heaped up in the interval by the regime of the Fascists—which many foreigners in London and Paris admired to the point of being bored by those who, like myself, predicted the bloody surprise which the Fascists were preparing then for Europe and for an unhappy Italy. It is by building upon the vital, healthy forces of the people

[1] Successively commanders-in-chief of the Allies at Salonika. The Italian army in Albania had fought as a separate entity, independent of Allied General Headquarters.

that the leaders of a free Italy will be able to work for the salvation of their country and of an organized Europe —on condition that they be neither conservatives without imagination and generosity or demagogues without honor and faith.

CHAPTER XI

The Italians and Their French Neighbors

SEVERAL TIMES in this book I have insisted on the distance between public opinion and a certain form of our literature. This is also true of the literature about Anglo-French relations, and we may add that quarrelsome political literature is quite out of harmony with the sentiments of the masses on both sides of the Alps.

Before 1940 a million Italians lived peacefully beside the French in the French regions of Savoy, Dauphiné, Provence, and Languedoc. In the part of maritime Provence where I have a house and a pine grove, Italians form half the population of villages for fifty miles around. Never does one hear of a dispute caused by difference of nationality. It has been the same elsewhere, from the sea to the Alps. This is why so many Frenchmen in these regions, during 1939–40, were so firmly convinced that Mussolini would not go to war against them.

This same assurance, we must add, was visible in Paris among the classes which call themselves "upper," but their reasons were infinitely less noble. These people thought, even if they did not dare say it, that this dictator whom they had touted so loudly, would have no reason to fight them, because he knew they admired him and envied the eternally discontented, democratic Italians for having a "good dictator."

Among French writers—not to antedate the fascist pe-

riod—those who admired Mussolini always added a touch
of antipathy for the Italian people, whereas those who attacked fascism were unsuccessful in hiding their opinion
—proved lamentably false since 1940, that the French people would never put up a single day with a dictatorship so
heavy, so cruel, and so vulgar.

The French writers who have tried to put their compatriots on guard against the allegedly permanent hatreds
and rancors of the Italians against the French, have never
been able to offer as proof any but literary names, never
a popular gesture. These literary names were moreover always the same: Alfieri and his *Misogallo*, Gioberti and his
Primato, Crispi, Mazzini—two Piedmontese, a Sicilian,
and a Ligurian. God be praised that they did not add the
name of the immortal Tuscan, Dante, because of the question which he asks of Virgil in the tenth division of the
eighth circle of Hell: "Was there ever a people as vain as
the Sienese? Even the French are not so full of vanity."

Without setting the list of the incriminated against the
names of great Italians who, like Manzoni and Carducci,
always had a profound liking for the things and ideas of
France, I shall consider only the four cases mentioned in
this myth, all of whom except Crispi were writers. And I
make no excuse for continuing to talk about writers; they
are representative, even in spite of themselves. When Ber-
nardin de Saint-Pierre asked Rousseau if Saint-Preux were
not himself, Jean-Jacques replied: "No. Saint-Preux is not
exactly what I have been, but what I would like to have
been." Writers are more profoundly true in what they represent than in their material reality.

Alfieri's *Misogallo* was a collection of virulent epigrams

against the French of the Revolution. But this same Alfieri, who was in Paris in 1789 for the publication of his tragedies by Didot, had greeted the fall of the Bastille with an enthusiastic ode. He was a republican, suspicious of Louis XVI and of the "Autrichienne." In all his tragedies the most likable heroes are the king-haters. But he was *Count* Alfieri, much more so than he thought; his mistress was the daughter of the Prince of Stolberg, separated wife of the Count of Albany, who was the chief of the Stuart dynasty. All these titles had small appeal for the Committees of 1793, who expelled Alfieri, in spite of his republicanism and his July 14 ode, and confiscated his goods. Alfieri's hatred was inspired even more by disillusionment than by desire to get even. The *Misogallo* was his safety valve, and it is well known that after giving vent to his feelings an Italian forgets. No one was ever more Italian than Alfieri. Vengeance, which the good but clumsy Walter Scott calls "the cold meat of the Italians," is the stock-in-trade of the dullest French and English writers. After his *Misogallo*— which he promptly forgot—Alfieri established himself in Florence, busied himself studying Greek, sulked at the Russians and the Sans-Culottes alike, and snickered at the idea of Bonaparte being presented to the world as an ancient hero, even though he scorned still more the impotent fury of the legitimists. He died in Florence in 1803. France later had the good luck to take perfect vengeance for the *Misogallo:* the most important souvenirs of Alfieri—manuscripts and portraits—are piously kept at Montpellier.

The one or two French writers of each generation who discover the tirades of Alfieri against the "Francesi" never suspect that they are the only ones who read them and that

they would look more like accomplished students of Italy
if they added that the *Misogallo* has fallen into almost complete oblivion among Italians. For example, Lauro de
Bosis, the young Italian poet who perished in 1931 when
he was dropping anti-fascist leaflets on Rome from an
airplane, did not include in his posthumously published
Golden Book of Italian Poetry, which is certainly the most
complete and objective anthology we have ever had, a single anti-French verse of Alfieri.

The case of Gioberti is different. This muddled little
Piedmontese *abbé* was stifling in the police-ridden Turin of
King Charles-Albert. Whatever breadth of mind he had
came largely from the twelve years he spent as an exile,
from 1833 to 1845, in France and Belgium. But he felt no
gratefulness toward France; he was a philosopher, and
philosophers are even more irascible than men of letters.
France had, for him, the fault of having invented and
launched the philosophy of sensism. French philosophers
from Descartes to Condorcet were his personal enemies. He
invented, or thought he invented, a new philosophy, and he
finally came to think that that philosophy was an exclusive
privilege of Italy and that he, Gioberti, had the mission of
defending that privilege. Hence the hodge-podge of his
Primato morale e civile degli Italiani (1843), in which,
after claiming for the papacy the moral domination of the
world as practiced in the time of the Gregories and Inno-
cents, he affirms that the supremacy of Italy is evident because the seat of the papacy . . . and so forth.

This book, appearing on the eve of the great explosion of
1848, had the fate it deserved: the pages which demonstrated the possibilities of a renaissance awakened a pro-

found echo in the Italians who were struggling for Italy. But the rest went unknown, the philosophical system as well as the attacks upon neighboring peoples. "Gioberti" rightly remains among the names of Italians who helped to form the atmosphere of the *Risorgimento*. But his work has left nothing deep or valid in the Italian mind. De Sanctis, the most independent and powerful Italian critic of the whole nineteenth century, was probably thinking of Gioberti's attacks upon France and the French when he wrote: "In Gioberti a simple heat of the imagination dominates. Where he accumulates his most outrageous epithets, you are tempted to step backward out of the way, afraid of meeting such a furious fellow. But have no fear. All that is mere verbiage; there are no profound ideas behind it. He is neither thinker nor statesman."

Moreover, in his *Rinnovamento,* written after the trials and failures of 1848, Gioberti himself repudiated almost everything he had adored when he wrote the *Primato:* the Piedmontese state, the pope, the Guelph programs.

Crispi's long life belonged to the two generations following. His name has probably had much to do with the not unbiased judgments which French historians have passed on the Italian policies of the period of the Triple Alliance. In truth, the only fault of the erstwhile Sicilian conspirator was an intellectually immature, emotive temperament. I can still hear Giolitti, in his humble orchard at Cavour, telling me how surprised he was when, at the time when he was Treasury Minister under Crispi, the latter called him in one fine morning at daybreak to confide to him a terrible secret: the French had decided to seize Spezia. And to his dying day Crispi congratulated himself that for the good of

Italy a man of his kidney had been in power at such a dangerous moment. In reality there had been nothing in it. For the Sicilian Crispi, the occupation of Tunis in 1881 had been a deep wound; it was this—the way it was done as well as the fact itself—that put him perpetually on the alert where the French were concerned. But was it not a president of the French Republic who replied to Bismarck's offer to aid France to go into Tunisia: "Does that clodhopper want us to get in bad once and for all with the Italians?" The sad fact is that in politics it is so much easier to remember only the wrongs committed by others.

The truth is that, the Crispi period aside, the Triple Alliance was always used by Italy as a simple assurance of peace, to guarantee territorial integrity and the status quo in the Mediterranean.

It is in a dispatch of Visconti-Venosta, one of the most enlightened of the predecessors of Crispi—a secret dispatch and consequently one which reveals unvarnished the ideas of the Italian State—that the sentiment with which Italy later acceded to the Alliance with Germany and Austria-Hungary is most clearly defined.

If war should be provoked by the folly or imprudence of France, or if it should come out of the clerical question, our position would be clear and we would share a common and direct interest with the Germans. But if there should be war as a result of the considered decision of Germany to attack France, Italy would be unable to participate in the war on the side of Germany; she would appear, not as an ally, but as an assassin working for a price. Besides, the results of a war between France and Germany would always be dangerous and harmful to Italy. If Germany were once more to crush France, she would want to end it with a dismemberment which she would wrongly consider definitive—one of those excessive, artificial, and therefore ephemeral plans, on the model of those which Napoleon used for making and breaking his peace treaties. Now, Italy would have neither strength nor future in a Europe which had lost its equilibrium.

I have published this document because, despite the difference of time and situation, the far-sighted words of the old Italian liberal statesman apply, unfortunately, to the war-mad policies which Mussolini adopted against France when she had been flattened by a new German invasion, seventy years later.

It is not without significance, I might add parenthetically, that these words of Viconti-Venosta foreshadow the definition "a stab in the back" that Franklin D. Roosevelt gave in June, 1940, of Mussolini's aggression against a France which her military leaders had decided not to defend. The Italians (not in Italy, they knew better there) who in the United States resented Roosevelt's words as an offense to Italy will be surprised to discover that Visconti —the disciple of Mazzini and Cavour—used even stronger words when he envisaged an unprovoked Italian war against France on the side of Germany. In reality it was not Roosevelt who offended Italy, but those Italians and Italo-Americans who identified our country with the gang of adventurers in power.

Even to a sovereign name like that of Mazzini, French writers have often thought that they could apply the stupid adjective, "Francophobe." As if, on the moral heights on which Mazzini moved there remained any place for national hatreds! The most celebrated of French magazines, the *Revue des deux mondes*, which spoke of Mazzini at the time of his death as sixty years later people spoke of the Bolsheviks, never mentioned his name without adding that "this dangerous revolutionary hated France." The truth was the exact contrary.

At Rome, in 1849, Mazzini saw his dearest friends fall under the fire of the French, but from the Capitol, where he sat as Triumvir of the Roman Republic, he decreed on May 7, 1849:

Whereas there is not, nor can there be, a state of war between the French people and Rome; and

Whereas Rome has the right and duty to defend her own inviolability, while deploring as a crime against the common faith any offense of one republic toward the other; and

Whereas the Roman people does not hold responsible for the acts of a mistaken government the soldiers who fought in obedience to orders;

The Triumvirate decrees:

Article 1. The Frenchmen made prisoner by our arms are herewith set at liberty and returned to the French camp.

Was this mere political cleverness in dealing with a heavily superior enemy? Perhaps—Mazzini demonstrated throughout the life of the Roman Republic that it is not necessary to be an adventurer in order to govern with political cleverness. But the decree of 1849 reflected his real desires. Here is what he wrote seventeen years earlier, in 1832, in an address to German youth:

Men of Germany, establish your nationality truly and with honor, and none will rise to menace it. Then only will you have the right not to count among your obstacles a people which has worked so vigorously for the whole of Europe. This people, dragged on by a despot, invaded you. Yet, even then, France brought you improvement and left you greatly better off than you were before.

These words were certainly not in the tradition of the treaties of Westphalia. But is it so sure that the policies of the Westphalia treaties have in the long run been fruitful for France?

Forty years later, in 1871, after the Prussian victory, Mazzini's explanation of these victories made a deep impression in Italy and England.

Because of conditions inherent in the system and because of the obligation under which the Empire found itself to use the army as an instrument, not of the nation, but of a tottering party, the Empire and the Empire alone is responsible for these facts: that the *soldier,* naturally heroic, has felt dwindling within himself the conscience and the enthusiasm of the *citizen;* and that even when that conscience has not given way, the bond between the soldier and the chief has loosened; now, without this bond, no victory is possible. Under the Empire, military chiefs were chosen not for their merit but according to the virulence of their Bonapartism, and, at most, according to the dubious results of the Algerian campaigns. These men knew that there would be need of them to subjugate the country. That is why they acquired, perhaps in spite of themselves, the habits of praetorians; corruption filtered into the army almost as it had in Russia.

The soldier, who is a more watchful and freer observer in France than he is elsewhere, quickly devined all that. His confidence in his chiefs abated.

Founded on corruption, the Second Empire was to perish by corruption. The reports that Louis-Napoleon received from his armies were frequently untrue. And equally mendacious were those who described the South Germans as ready to rise against the Prussians.

And further on, in a passage which calls to mind the stupid enterprises undertaken fifty years later in the Palatinate and the Ruhr by Poincaré:

The immense sums wasted among the German Catholics of the Rhineland in trying to persuade them to pronounce in favor of France more than once found their way into the pockets of secret agents. Besides, it is not by means of this type that one can kill the national sentiment of a people.

And finally:

Faithless plagiarist of his uncle, Louis-Napoleon never verified things; he simply believed. When, after his arrival in the midst of his army, truth opened his eyes, it was too late. Having declared war and chosen the moment for attack, he found himself forced back on the defensive, incapable of marching on Mainz, incapable of operating by way of Strasbourg in southern Germany . . . incapable even of destroying the nearest centers of the German railroads. Inert, motionless, he awaited the attack, and he was beaten. The traditional valor of the French soldier again came into its own, but it could not suffice alone against such unfavorable conditions as the incompetence of the chiefs had succeeded in building up.

This severe but just criticism of a dictatorial regime was the most favorable thing published regarding France in 1871 in any neutral country. At the end of the same piece, turning toward Germany, Mazzini added:

Guided by a predatory monarchy, Germany abandoned the ways of justice and truth. She has created an atmosphere of vengeance which bears the germs of future wars. May God and the nations beware of it. And may France soon regain the influence to which she has a right, and some day aid Germany (as our people avenged themselves for the siege of Rome by going to fall for France at Dijon) to fashion a germanic national unity based upon liberty.

Precisely because this language is not flat and saccharine, it is profoundly friendly. Mazzini had the soul of a prophet, and his language is so fair that I know some Frenchmen will recognize in it their own feelings after the victory of 1918 and perhaps even, in part, after their defeat of 1940—as for instance the passage where Mazzini insists upon the traditional valor of the French soldier and

the incompetence of the generals. What France lacked after
the ephemeral intoxication of the treaty of Versailles was,
not the clear-sightedness of her best men, but the courage to oppose openly the Panglossian optimism of those
who wanted to make France believe that the provisions of
any treaty are sufficient. I could give a thousand examples
of that state of mind, drawn from my embassy to France
in 1922. An episode which took place on the first day of
my mission is enough. On presenting my credentials to
President Millerand, I delivered the little discourse which
is conventional at such times, expressing the hope of being
able to count upon his support for everything which I desired to further in the interest of our two countries, including, I added, a fruitful understanding between France and
Italy to the end of organizing Europe. President Millerand
replied that like myself he considered it necessary to work
for "the organization of peace in the *world*." By substitut-
ing "world" for "Europe," the French government put
away as too dangerous the idea that Briand later took up
again—too late—of the urgent necessity of creating common ties, political and economic, between the different
states of Europe.

Probably certain narrow and suspicious minds in certain
old Parisian *salons* and in certain corners of the Academy
found me a dubious friend, since I dared to talk about
something which resembled a "United States of Europe"—
a formula which I have never used, by the way, because it
is too formalistic and mechanical.

Certainly the resemblance between the cultured and aristocratic classes in Italy and in France is not so marked
as that between the masses. The life, and in a large meas-

ure, the thought of the common people in Savoy, Piedmont, Languedoc, and Tuscany are identical. However, the intellectual formation at the top of the pyramid is very different, even from the psychological point of view; we are not only unendowed with the cartesian clarity of French intellectualism, but also blind enough not to complain about it.

The same is true of political culture. The conservative mandarins of France are the ones who are most distant from us. All in all, the old gentlemen of the French Academy and of the *Revue des deux mondes* discovered their ardent admiration for Italy only when her dearest traditions were raped and torn by the policed violence of Mussolini's regime. These surviving specimens of a Charles X past thus admitted unwittingly how little they felt and loved the permanent virtues of the Italian character.

CHAPTER XII

The Italians and Their Swiss Neighbors

IF WE were to judge fascism simply by its relations with the Swiss Confederation, we should have to conclude that Mussolini and his regime were more to be pitied for their stupidity than censured for their crimes. Happily they did not succeed, but, secretly or openly as occasion offered, they tried to stir up a national awakening in Italian Switzerland. And yet even the Fascists should have been able to see that the Italian cantons in the Swiss Federation were absolutely necessary for the continued existence of Switzerland. It is almost inconceivable that the French-speaking Swiss and the Germanic Swiss could go on living together without their Italian confederates. This is as much as to say that Mussolini tried to give the whole of Switzerland from Lucerne to Zurich to the Reich, in return for the dubious pleasure of annexing the poor cantons of Ticino and Grisons, whose Italian populations are so much more useful to us as representatives of the Italian tongue and culture in the bosom of the most cosmopolitan and central of all the states of Europe.

"You speak our language, therefore you belong to us," cried (or, when appropriate, whispered) the Fascists to the Swiss of Ticino and Grisons. The more naïve of the Fascists thought they were carrying on the work of the Italian *Risorgimento,* which had succeeded in reuniting in one body almost all Italians, from the Alps to Sicily. Perhaps the Fascists did not suspect that Mazzini on one hand and Cavour on the other appealed more to the will to freedom than to feelings of blood and race. The Italians of the thousand-year-old republic of San Merino, in the very center of Italy, were determined to keep their old statutes and their old flag. Free Italy permitted them to do so.

Switzerland is the living proof that the miracle of a happy national life is worked more by the free consent of the population than by language, natural frontiers, or religion. Switzerland has within its borders three languages, German, French, and Italian—even four if one counts Latin. All the confederated peoples cling to the literary traditions of their languages, but they cling just as closely to the maintenance of their Union, their common laws, and their parliament at Berne.

Swiss citizens, whether Italian, French, or German, have in common the conviction that not only the bureaucracy but the state itself belongs to them. There is none of the servility which the German shows when he deals with even the most minor functionary of the *Reich*. Nor is there any of the passivity of the French toward the "Administration." The Swiss, whether he is from Lugano or Lucerne, never feels that he has to tolerate an abuse—a feeling, we must admit, in which he is aided by the smallness of his country, which permits him to know everyone, including not only the Council of his Canton but also the personnel of the Federal Departments at Berne.

Each canton is a genuine country. Ask any Swiss point-blank where he comes from. He will never tell you that he is Swiss without saying first, each in his own language: "I am from Vaud," or, "I am from Ticino," or, "I am from

Berne." Hence a happy condition which is lacking in
France and in England and even to a certain degree in the
United States. Every Swiss city still preserves an astonishing vitality, just as was always the case with the cities of
free Italy.

In France talent rushes to Paris, empoverishing Dijon
and Bordeaux, Toulouse and Lille, those centers which
were so alive during the eighteenth century; in England
everyone hastens to London, even—or especially—the
Scots; in the United States fortune and glory are to be
sought in New York.

If we consider only Italian Switzerland, ideas and expressions at Lugano differ from those at Bellinzona, hardly
an hour distant, to such an extent that one can say that the
ancient and very particularist Italy of our grandfathers remains nowhere so alive as in the canton of Ticino.

This is why the existence and proximity of a federal
Switzerland constitutes a model of nonstandardized living
for the Italians of Italy. As for the international diplomatic
advantage which Switzerland offers Italy, the facts are so
evident that it is difficult to understand how even the Fascists failed to see them. In the approximately normal Europe which existed before the aggressions of Hitler, the
Italian-Swiss frontier represented for Italy a long bound-
ary fully as secure as the Canadian frontier is for the
United States.

Outside Italy, even in the countries where the government of Berne had no diplomatic representatives, the Swiss
who lived there as technicians or manufacturers or merchants were authorized to enlist the aid of the offices of the
embassies of Italy or France or Germany, each according
to his individual taste.

Swiss are very numerous in Italy, especially at Milan
and Genoa. They meet for the rare Swiss holidays, but
otherwise, in the ordinary run of life, they mix so well
with the Italians that no one ever thinks of them as foreigners.

This is almost as true of the Swiss Minister at Rome.
When as Foreign Minister I received a foreign representative, I never forgot where he came from, even if he spoke
my language. But with the Swiss Minister I found it natural to talk of Italian problems as if he were a compatriot;
and I was not imprudent. Every responsible Swiss is anxious, and should be anxious, to maintain the political and
spiritual strength of Italy, just as every Italian should repeat about Switzerland—and with warmer enthusiasm—
the phrase some diplomat uttered regarding the Austria-
Hungary of Franz-Joseph: "If it did not exist, someone
would have had to invent it."

The more we talk of a federated Europe, the more we
should be concerned not to stifle—if ever it were possible
to stifle—the marvelous wealth of our national civiliza-
tions beneath a standardization which threatens already to
stupefy the whole of Germany. Even without the extreme
example of Nazi slavery one cannot deny that the economic prosperity of certain supernational groups, like the
former Austria-Hungary, or "uni-national" ones, like the
United States, has been bought sometimes at the price of
an intellectual leveling process which threatened to lower
the worth of the individuals concerned. The autonomous
rights of the Swiss cantons should be a living lesson to
us all.

Napoleon I, that Italian who was so fatal for France because he won almost all the battles and lost all the wars,

displayed in Switzerland what he also displayed in Italy, Poland, and Spain, his incapacity to understand the soul of a people. He imposed on the Swiss people a Helvetic republic, "one and indivisible." It did not, because it could not, last. To the Swiss, centralization would be slavery.

Indeed, the earlier political history of the Swiss cantons proved that it was necessary to submit particularism to a superior law; it will be the same in the Europe of the future. The Federal constitution of 1848 made the cantons subordinate to a common law governing the supreme common interests. But at the same time, an attempt was made to safeguard the rights and independence of the cantons.

The same was true of the revision of the constitution of 1874, which accorded more authority to the Federal government, as a result of the alarm caused among the Swiss by the Franco-Prussian war. I have examined a collection of contemporary newspapers of Ticino, little sheets from Lugano, Locarno, and Bellinzona. The articles and opinions would have done honor to any of the great newspapers of Europe. The citizens of Ticino were even better aware than were people in Zurich and Geneva that while it was necessary to defend local liberties, within well-defined limits they would have to accept, in order to defend them, a common superior authority.

As good Swiss and good Italians, they showed themselves to be imbued with the international spirit which has always remained so vital among the compatriots of Dante and Mazzini—the international spirit of which fascism will only have effected a shameful, but temporary, eclipse.

CHAPTER XIII

The Italians and Their German Neighbors

ALL EDUCATED MEN know that one of the most constant traditions of the great Italian universities has been to call in learned foreigners, even for chairs in which Italians might have been better. Through three generations of struggle against the Germans—struggles whose moral center was in the universities—Italians were always anxious to maintain the closest contact with German culture. This was an essential trait of the nineteenth-century Italian mind.

The historians, philosophers, and philologians of 1821, 1831, 1848, 1859, and 1860 interrupted their studies of Fichte and Hegel only to go and fight or conspire against the German hegemony. In the prison of Castel dell'Ovo, at Naples, De Sanctis translated the works of Hegel into Italian. About the same time Alessandro Poerio, the poet-hero killed by a German bullet during the war of 1848, vaunted "the cosmopolitanism of the mind" as the ideal of the Italian thought of his generation.

The common people shared these ideas. Niccolini would be a forgotten poet if all Italians had not repeated, from 1848 to 1918: "Ripassin l'Alpe et tornerem fratelli [Let them go back beyond the Alps and we shall again be brothers]." The letters of our soldiers, especially the officers, to their families during the war of 1914–18 are full of human sympathy when they describe meetings with the

German and Hungarian prisoners and wounded. From the front near Gorizia my elder brother Cesare wrote me one day:

I can no longer read pages full of hatred [and yet he had enlisted of his own free will]; I feel nothing but pity for those poor devils of Tyroleans and Styrians we kill off every day. Yesterday I tried to repeat to myself the *Sant'Ambrogio* of Giusti that we learned by heart when we were children. If you have a Giusti there in Corfu, send it to me.

Giusti had written his *Sant'Ambrogio* in 1846, at the height of the Austrian oppression. He described in it the "slow, slow German hymn" which the soldiers of the oppressor's garrison raised to God in the old church of Sant' Ambrogio; he admitted the "bitter sadness" which had seized his heart as he listened.

> Hatred that ever holds asunder
> The Lombard from the German nation
> Serves him who ruling keeps them parted
> Fearing their reconciliation.

In a Europe brutalized by years of fascist and nazi dictatorship—and even after the fall of the dictatorships —it would be harder to find a Giusti to write a new *Sant'Ambrogio*. And it would be as hard to find a gesture like that of Manzoni, who dedicated his war hymn against the Austrians to "Theodore Koerner, a name dear to all who struggle to reconquer their fatherland."

Fascism, in its work of degrading the Italians, even produced some who in their intellectual innocence believed that they accentuated their Italianism by copying with enthusiasm the racial and nationalistic theories which are contrary to the highest traditions of Italian thought. But it is also true that the malady was, or appeared to be, more

or less universal. In Paris the Academician Claude Far-
rère decreed that Victor Hugo was an "imbecile." In Germany, a Theodore Koerner would have ended in a concen-
tration camp unless, like Thomas Mann, he managed to
escape from the country.

The Italian people took an interest in the German people
as such only during the most serious crisis through which
the Germans have ever passed, the Reformation, a crisis
in comparison with which nazism will eventually seem
only a bloody side show. Being deeply respectful of every
sincere expression of religious feeling, I should be sorry to
shock even a follower of Luther. But how can it be denied
that the Lutheran revolt ended by plunging the German
people into dangerous isolation and irremediable servitude
to its temporal masters? We must take up the study of
Luther again if we want to understand Hitler better. Luther
prepares the way for Hitler's race theories when he writes
in his *Table Talk:* "We Germans are Germans, we will remain Germans," a formula which is righteous enough, especially for a people deprived by geography of frontiers
like those of Italy and Spain. The danger emerges when
Luther adds that there is a "German nature" which alone
possesses "force of character, perseverance in labor, mod-
eration in manners, faithfulness, magnanimity . . ." in
short "the best of peoples of all times, the nation *par excel-
lence.*" As for the other countries, the sound is one which
we hear four centuries later in *Mein Kampf:* the Italians
have nothing but "grace," the French are only "eloquent,"
and the Russians are treated as if this were already the
Nazi Conference at Nurnberg, 1936: "They are hardly the
equals of the Turks."

Mein Kampf is forecast by Luther when he tries to

demonstrate that force in the service of "justice" should not be limited. These pages are singularly reminiscent of the Hitlerian theory of 1936, that the German people alone has the right to judge whether or not it has violated a treaty. For Luther war is only in appearance "a non-Christian activity and an offense against Christian Love. War which punishes the wicked . . . is an excellent and divine thing."

We can see how, according to the remark of Doellinger, the German people recognizes in Luther its own nature, *ihr potenziertes Selbst,* and that Hegel, Fichte, and Treitschke are his children. Professors of Treitschke's type bear the most guilt for poisoning German minds and betraying the ideas of Goethe. There was nothing strange in their struggle to turn Prussianism into Germanism, or that they should have given way after 1848–49 and again after 1866. They had to accept the Prussian solution to the German problem. Facts were facts. But they did not limit themselves to this; like Treitschke they adored what they had once vituperated. They no longer believed in anything but the "Power" which characterized the period of Bismarck and the Williams, and later they believed only in the fever of Hitlerism. If they had remained a respectful but reasonable opposition, they would have been of invaluable service in maintaining the mental equilibrium of their country.

These men thought that they were being political realists by surrendering to immorality and shutting humanity out of their souls. Actually they were so clumsy that even their hero, Bismarck, made cruel sport of them. They became mere "experts" in science or philology, just as the politicians acquiesced in becoming nothing more than the errand boys of the administration.

Everyone—the learned as well as the politicians—forgot that nothing great or durable for a country ever can come out of narrow nationalism and that those countries alone are great which, like the France of the *Encyclopédie* or the Italy of the *Risorgimento*—and like what Kant and Goethe hoped that Germany might be—have a message of consequence for the world.

The Italian people have never ceased to feel these things instinctively. It has at times been said that they detested the Austrians and bore no grudge against the Germans. On the contrary, the Italians felt that the imperial system of the Hapsburgs gravely menaced their development, but they had no antipathy toward the Austrians who, after all, had been molded by so many Italian influences. After a period of hopes and illusions, they felt the greatest antipathy against the Germans of learned, Lutheran Germany, because, while still recognizing the remarkable qualities of German "experts" and technicians, the Italians felt the Germans to be so lacking in that humane fellow feeling without which one never gets to the hearts of my compatriots.

CHAPTER XIV

The Italians and Their Yugoslav Neighbors

THROUGHOUT THE HISTORY of our country two types of man have persisted. One is the realistic thinker who draws his philosophy from cold observation of social life. Machiavelli, who opened the period of modern thought in Italy and whose true character was so different from the conventional conception of Machiavellianism formed by superficial foreigners, was of this type. So were Cavour, the best-rounded statesman of the nineteenth century, and Giolitti (only yesterday), with his somewhat pragmatic simplicity and hatred for empty phrases. The other is the type of the humane saint, from Saint Francis down to Saint Philip Neri, Mazzini, the brothers Bandiera who were shot down by the Bourbons of Naples, Mameli the young hero-poet killed by a French ball at the siege of Rome in 1849, Battisti the Trentinese. There is also a third type, fortunately sporadic, which Battisti scorned because he had known it so closely at Trent, the demagogue blown up either by sterile hatreds or with a pseudo-Roman thirst for glory, Mussolini.

The two great classic types of Italian genius agreed throughout the nineteenth century about the problems of our immediate neighbors to the east, the South Slavs. It is useful to draw attention to this agreement in political thought. In the first half of the nineteenth century our Slavic neighbors, at the dawn of their national awakening, found in Mazzini the first and most eloquent defender of their ideals. In his *Lettere slave* Mazzini established the European importance of the Yugoslav problem. All Italians are familiar with these letters—or at least were familiar until the ideas of Mazzini were repudiated by the fascist regime.

What is less well known is that a few years later Cavour, an Italian of the opposite type from Mazzini, also wrote about the South Slavs with just as much sympathy. It was in the midst of the Italian war against the Austria of Radetzky; the Croats were fighting in the plains of Lombardy with a loyalty to the Hapsburg dynasty that was later repaid by an example of Hapsburg ingratitude which "astonished the world," even the world of the other sovereigns—which is saying much.

In his newspaper Cavour told the Italians: "It is vain and useless for you to hate the Croats; like you they are victims of an egoistic power which sets one against the other its subjects, with their eleven languages. Some day these Croats, with their Slavic brothers of the south, should be the best friends and allies of a free Italy . . ."

I still have a vivid memory of the long walks I took at Corfu during the war with Prince Alexander, the future first King of Yugoslavia. We were at the end of the old Venetian road of Cannone, in a pine grove opposite the Isle of Ulysses. I mentioned to him the letters on the Slavs written by Cavour in 1848. Knowing Mazzini's *Lettere slave* but not the writings of Cavour, he asked me for them. And as I did not have them at Corfu, although the house where I had installed my legation had a very fine Italian library, I had them sent from Rome and forwarded to him at Salonika, where he had gone in the meantime. His reply was the brief letter, written in French, which follows:

My dear Count,

I thank you very sincerely for your friendly gift and the words which accompany it. The ideas of Cavour should sometime become reality. My respects to Countess Sforza. I hope that your children are withstanding the privations of Corfu.

Believe me, yours . . .

I am as sure today as I was then that what he said about the ideas of Cavour was sincere. He knew how convinced I was of the necessity of a fruitful understanding between our two peoples after the House of Hapsburg should fall —a fall of which I never doubted even in the most trying moments of the war—and he shared my view. I have spent so much time with Alexander Karageorgevich, at moments when there was no place for diplomatic attitudinizing, that I am able to affirm that he never ceased to want a true understanding between our peoples, as the one way of assuring the definitive well-being and security of his country.

For my part, even when—thinking his course was right —he set out on a dictatorship which I dared tell him he would find a blind alley, I never forgot the loyalty and fervor with which he had always tried to further everything which could serve the cause of Italo-Yugoslav friendship —a cause which was so dear, a century ago, to the hearts and minds of two great Italians, Mazzini and Cavour.

An Italy secure in its true strength and vitality should want even more: that the ancient animosities between the Serbs and the Bulgars give way to a relationship which may some day become the nucleus of a free union of the South Slavs. As Foreign Minister I had a chance to see what evil and uninspired policy, with no confidence in its own strength, could do. My predecessor, Sonnino, as well-intentioned as he was limited, had thought of the war as an exclusively Austro-Italian struggle, and he wanted to avoid killing Austria. He had not understood that the extinction of the Hapsburg Empire was the stake we were playing for. Austria having disappeared, he inherited her old, narrow ideas, especially that of playing off the Balkan countries against each; several other Italian diplomats finally shared his view. When, not long afterward, I urged in one of my dispatches that they work for a reconciliation of Bulgars and Serbo-Croato-Slovenes, I felt so much confused hesitation in their replies that I called them all to Rome. I said: "Are you all followers of the Hapsburgs, to conceive the strength of Italy in the Balkans to reside only in the Austrian 'divide and rule'? The better the Yugoslavs manage to unite with other Slavs, just as the Yugoslavs themselves have united, the more seas they will have access to. Thus we shall be more secure in the Adriatic and have more influence in the Balkans."

Italian suspiciousness of our Slavic neighbors could only befit a people who did not feel sure of their power of intellectual, political, and spiritual expansion. Thus it was natural that this sickly anti-Slav sentiment should exist in the Fascists, who, like the Nazis, are only the product of a morbid "inferiority complex." Speaking for their benefit I once declared in the Chamber at Rome: "You want barbed wire to the east because you live only on fear and suspicion. I, on the contrary, want all to be open, because I am sure of the force of Italy's moral and economic expansion."

Since that time the errors and crimes of the Fascists

against the permanent interests of Italy have piled up. An example is that baroque and artificial "Realm of Croatia," invented in Rome in 1941 and approved by Hitler, who knew that without the unity of the Yugoslavs, as without the independence of the Czechs,[1] Italy remains the more at the mercy of a victorious Germany. But all that will pass; left to themselves, the Italians and the South Slavs have no reason to do anything but understand each other. As I declared on a solemn occasion to the Italian Parliament: "If not for love, then out of necessity and self-interest, the two peoples will have to work together." [2]

[1] For this problem I refer the reader to my last book to appear in unconquered France: *Synthèse de l'Europe*, Paris, Gallimard.

[2] For a closer view of Italo-Slavic relations see my *Fifty Years of Wars and Diplomacy in the Balkans* (New York, Columbia University Press, 1941) and certain chapters of my *Makers of Modern Europe* (London, Elkins and Marrott), and my *Frères ennemis* (Paris, Gallimard).

CHAPTER XV

The Italians and Their English Neighbors

THE ITALIANS and the English would be neighbors even if the story that Voltaire tells in one of his smaller works were untrue. An Englishman, says Voltaire, seated in his gondola in Venice, dipped a finger in the Grand Canal and then, having tasted the water, sat back. "Ah, it's salt. Well, here I am in England."

The two peoples have mixed too often. Their intellectual relations have been too intimate. In spite of the war which Mussolini declared on England in 1940, a people is always friendly with the neighbor of a neighbor. This psychological law will stay true even when all the nations of Europe are united in more or less close bonds, federal and economic.

Besides, if the English and Germans have never understood each other very well—the weak attempts of Queen Victoria and her Prince Consort can be said to have counted for little—the principal reason is that while the English are for the most part of Teutonic and Scandinavian origin a majority of their words and the strength and spirit of their literature are of Latin and Italian extraction. Mind was stronger than blood. Shakespeare—whom the Germans sometimes claim as a German poet—is full of Italian ideas which were the glass of fashion and the mold of form in the London of his time.

A generation after Shakespeare, Milton wrote in Ital-

ian. Gladstone read our poets constantly. He had a profound admiration for Leopardi, who said in the poem he
addressed to his sister after her marriage in 1821:

> Know that thy sons must be
> Wretched or craven. Choose the first . . .[1]

When, in 1821, the Carbonari of Naples revolted against
the Bourbon King, Shelley wrote his "Ode to Naples" in
scorn for the Austrian armies, those

> Earth-born Forms
> Arrayed against the ever-living Gods.

At about the same time Byron established intimate contact with the liberals who were conspiring in Romagna
against the regime of the popes. He waited anxiously for
the Naples revolution to extend from Ravenna to Bologna.
February 18, 1821, knowing that he was in danger, since
his house had become an arsenal and depot for the liberals,
he wrote ". . . to be sacrificed in case of accidents? It is
no great matter, supposing that Italy could be liberated,
who or what is sacrificed. It is a great object—the very
poetry of politics. Only think—a free Italy!"

But Italy did not manage to free herself in 1821. The
great effort took place only in 1848. The English poets and
historians were the only ones in Europe to treat with generosity the events of 'forty-eight, so rich in moral beauty and
so poor in political experience. Meredith's novel *Vittoria*
is not only a great prose-poem but also a penetrating history of the Italian people in one of its most impelling
periods. In Italy itself it should be studied more as the

[1] *The Poems of Leopardi,* translated by G. L. Blickerstreth, Cambridge,
The University Press, 1923, p. 167.

testimony of a witness, a historical source of the highest order.

The events of 1859 found British minds more reserved. The love of Italian liberty had become more general than ever, but the Italian alliance with Napoleon III aroused suspicion. It could be said of the best of the English in 1859, when the war in Lombardy began, that they desired the victory of the Piedmontese and the free Italian armies over the Austrians, but at the same time they wanted Franz-Joseph to defeat Napoleon III. When Napoleon abandoned the cause of Italian independence on the battlefield, England became unanimously pro-Italian. In this she was aided by the presence in power of farsighted and noble statesmen like Gladstone, Lord John Russell, and Palmerston, all three hated by the German subconscious of Queen Victoria.

At that time England offered magnanimous hospitality to the great Italian exiles, Mazzini, Saffi, Panizzi, Carlo Poerio, Lacaita, and others. It was to them, and to the esteem that their ideas and their persons commanded, that the growing English enthusiasm for Italy was due. How much misfortune would have been spared Europe if the two Chamberlains, Austen and Neville, had listened while there was still time to other Italians, fully as worthy and as honorable, like Salvemini and Sturzo who went to London for refuge against fascist persecution. And if the English diplomats in fascist Italy had been worthier successors of Cavour's friend Hudson, who understood Italy so well, instead of believing, as they did, because the true interests of Italy and England were the same, that Mussolini could ever take sides against another dictator.

Neither these diplomats nor their master at London,

Neville Chamberlain, beclouded as they were by their fear of a "red menace," which never existed in Italy, ever understood that dictators are bound to each other by a pact of satanic solidarity. Hitler in Berlin and Mussolini in Rome could not fail to feel that their grasp on permanent power was for each the supreme interest. Of little import, after that, in the eyes of Mussolini, were the lasting interests of the great people submitted to his domination.

Aside from the recent and short, but disastrous, period in which British policy preferred an Italian dictator to the Italian people, the unique thing in the relations between the two peoples is that whereas in nineteenth-century France only the so-called "advanced" minds loved Italy, to such a degree that in 1859 Napoleon III made war against the wishes of almost all the conservatives, in England, on the other hand, every stratum of the nation shared an ardent enthusiasm for the cause of liberty and independence in Italy. The lone exceptions were Victoria and her consort, Albert of Coburg, who was after all a German, enlightened and honest, but withal profoundly German. The English brewery workers who shortly after the wars of 1848 stoned the Austrian Marshal Haynau, who had wanted to put to fire and sword the citizens of heroic Brescia, represented England with much greater nobility than "dear Queen Victoria."

In the war which Mussolini declared on England in 1940, with neither historic nor moral justification, the lone fault of the Italian people was to have allowed liberty of speech and of the press to be completely taken from them, bit by bit, since 1926. What Italian, under the fascist tyranny, would have dared cite and reprint the moving letter which Garibaldi sent in 1845 to the workers of New-castle? "England is a great nation, foremost in human progress, enemy to despotism, the only safe refuge of the exile, friend of the oppressed; if ever England should be so circumstanced as to require the help of an ally, cursed be the Italian who would not step forward in her defense."

CHAPTER XVI

The Italians and America

IT IS JUST AS WELL that we do not know who invented the expression "melting pot." The metaphor is far from happy. One does not melt souls, traditions, and aspirations, no matter if they do come from Germany, Poland, and Scotland. The expression has done little to help the United States in the opinion of the world at large.

If present-day America does not seem to present the picture of happily integrated humanity that she might, blame the hasty and mechanical concept of the melting pot. A day will come when the American people will fuse together spiritually and culturally, and isolated groups of Italians, Germans, and Irish within the commonwealth will be only a memory. But this will be, not because these groups have repudiated their origins, but because they have felt the supreme moral beauty of a new nationality whose aim is to guide the world toward a life without hatred and without egoism. On that day—and not before —the last barrier between Mayflower Americans and Ellis Island Americans will have gone down. The older Americans will get credit for having founded and safeguarded America and for having given the world that message of superhuman hope, the Declaration of Independence. And the newer Americans will just as surely get credit for having made America aware of its new responsibilities and its wider obligations. This credit will be considerable, for no power is worthy to survive if it does not feel its responsibilities.

It is not without reason that newcomers, those who are in closest contact with the problems of the Old World, should settle in the cities. Three quarters of the citizens of New York were born abroad or are children of foreigners; in Chicago, Boston, Cleveland, San Francisco, and Minneapolis the proportion is above 50 percent; in Philadelphia it is a flat 50 percent. These places with historic names, or names which will become historic, are the ones in which American political thought is most active.

We could add that even in the heroic days of the Revolution eighteen of the signers of the Declaration of Independence were not of English stock. We have to admit that most of the time when immigrants say "we" they mean their national group, especially if their stock is Slavic, Irish, or German. We must except the descendants of the Germans of 1848 who preferred exile to the materialistic dictatorship of Bismarck, the direct ancestor of Hitler. But it is not always sure that when the Italian immigrant says "we" he does not often add to himself, "We in America," out of his interest in a land to which he has attached the fortunes, so fundamentally important to an Italian, of his family. Who could be more American than the arch-Italian Fiorello LaGuardia, unless it is Joe DiMaggio? Even in contributions to the historical formation of the United States the Italians can point to more names than certain other nationalities. In 1941 Franklin D. Roosevelt declared, "To Colonel Francesco Vigo, a patriot of Italian birth, the United States are indebted, next to Clark, for the liberation of the Northwest regions." Buffalo, the second city of the state of New York, was founded by an Italian, Paolo Busti. Three Italian generals, Palma di Cesnola, Ferrero, and Spinola, distinguished themselves in the War between the States.

Doctor Mazzei was born at Poggio a Cajano, near Florence, in 1730. Bored with the calm of eighteenth-century Tuscany, he practiced medicine first at Smyrna and then in London. Being a better psychologist than the Ministers of King George III, he felt the latent strength beneath the stirrings of the American colonies, and in 1773 he went to Virginia, where he became the friend of Thomas Jefferson. At Richmond, in a newspaper article, he wrote a line which shortly became famous: "All men are by nature created free and independent." Jefferson took up the phrase, along with several others from the writings of his Italian friend, and gave them immortality in the Declaration of Independence.

When, after years of intimate intellectual relations with Jefferson, Mazzei had to go unwillingly back to Europe, he wrote Madison in Italian: "I am on the point of leaving, but my heart will remain behind. When I think of my feelings on crossing the Potomac, I am ashamed of my weakness. I do not know what will happen when Sandy Hook drops from sight behind me. But I know that wherever I may go, I shall always struggle for the well-being and progress of my adopted country."

It is strange that fascist propagandists, so busy making poor Mussolini look like a legitimate successor to the Caesars, have never thought of the real reasons why the Italian immigrants of the United States have a right to be proud.

Some years ago I happened to be lecturing at a large American university. One of the distinguished physicians of the city and I struck up a friendship, and he invited me several times to go hunting with him at his country place. I felt that there was more than a chance similarity in the way the two of us looked at life, and one day I told him so. He was a bit embarrassed. "My grandfather came from Tuscany. His name was Mazzei; but when my father had made his money he moved to this city and changed his name to Mathews." (I have changed the anglicized name the least bit to avoid any further chance of embarrassing him.)

That was the moment for me to tell the friendly doctor about the Mazzei who had been the friend of Jefferson. I also told him how Mazzei had not only brought the germs of the liberal ideas which were then beginning to grow up in France and Italy, but also the seeds of some of the vegetables which today grace American tables. My new friend was simply overwhelmed. "You mean to say that I may be the descendant of Jefferson's friend, and here I am, thanks to my father's weakness, just one more Mathews among all the other Mathewses in the city directory?"

The cheap mania for changing Italian names so that they sound more Anglo-Saxon has disappeared, however, with the normal Americanization of many Italian names, especially since names like LaGuardia and DiMaggio have become just as American as the thousands of Thomases who were Tommasi, Whites who were "Bianchi," Popes who were "Papa," Browns who were "Bruni," and Abbots who were "Abate."

There was a time when there was good reason for anglicizing Italian names for the sake of pronunciation. There was no intention of falsifying anything when a family named Caboto settled in Boston, changed its name to Cabot, and became one of the oldest families in Massachusetts. That happened without anyone's thinking twice about it, just as when members of my own family who went to the seventeenth-century wars in France and Flanders—and who certainly had no reason to want to change their name—had their name changed for them to Sforce simply because it was easier to pronounce. But how many more-or-less well-known, more-recently-arrived Americans have, or have had, artificially transformed Italian names. The aeronautical expert Henry Woodhouse came to America as "Enrico Casalegno"; Jim Flynn, who knocked out Jack Dempsey, was baptized "Andrea Chiariglione"; the baseball star Ping Bodie was "Francesco Pizzola"; the actor Don Ameche was "Amici"; the singer Ponselle, "Ponzillo"; football coach Lou Little was "Luigi Piccolo"; and one could add thousands to the list. I remarked one day to the distinguished president of an American university that his ways of thinking reminded me of Benedetto Croce. The compliment, although not unjustified, was so great that he told me what, up to that time, he had neglected to mention. "But my father's name was really . . ." and he mentioned an Italian name so like his own that I would not care to repeat it here.

All these gentlemen, university presidents and athletes alike, must assume a heavy responsibility for the long wail about discrimination which has now disappeared but which filled two generations of Italian hearts with bitterness. Perhaps some day an American writer of Italian blood will do for the Italians of the old-time Little Italies what no

Irish-American writer has done for the earlier wave of immigration: give us a real description of these humble people among whom so many talents were wasted. Some trace of these poor lives remains in the half-bitter, half-joyous, Italo-American poems of the eighties and nineties, written in the jargon which was then standard in the downtown Italian section and in the Bronx. Here is a sonnet about the building-trades workers of the time before labor legislation:

> Vennero i bricchelieri [1] a cento a cento
> Tutta una ghenga [2] co'calli alle mani,
> Per far la casa di quaranta piani,
> Senza contare il ruffo [3] e il basamento.[4]
> Adesso par che sfidi il firmamento
> A onore e gloria degli Americani;
> Ma chi pensa ai grinoni,[5] ai paesani
> Morto di colpo senza sacramento?
> Che val se per disgrazia o per mistecca [6]
> Ti sfracelli la carne in fondo al floro? [7]
> Povero ghinni,[8] disgraziato dego [9] . . .
> Davanti a mezzo ponte [10] di bistecca [11]
> Il bosso [12] ride e mostra il dente d'oro:
> "Chi e morto e morto. Io vivo e me no frego."

A group of young Italo-American novelists has already begun to exploit the rich field of the Americanization of Italian families. One is John Fante, author of *Wait until Spring, Bandini, Ask the Dusk, Dago Red*. Fante is the son of an Italian from Abruzzi and of an Italo-American mother. Another is Guido d'Agostino, born in New York of Sicilian parents, who wrote *Olives on the Apple Tree*.

[1] Bricklayers.	[2] Gang.	[3] Roof.	[4] Basement.
[5] Greenhorns.	[6] Mistake.	[7] Floor.	[8] Guineas.
[9] Dago.	[10] Pound.	[11] Beefsteak.	[12] Boss.

A young woman, Maria Tommasi, who wrote *Deep Grow the Roots*, was born in Vermont, and her parents were Piedmontese. Still others, like Joe Pagano and Pietro di Donato, have written novels which are remarkable for their rich lyricism and their deep observation of life. Not one of these young writers complains about "discrimination," since American critics have greeted and continue greeting their works with sympathetic interest.

It is curious that all these writers, born in America, have without exception obeyed the law which has governed Italian literature under fascism. All those who possess some talent—something more than the rhetorical facility which is the great weakness of the mediocre Italian—have spurned fascist phraseology and remained faithful to the traditions of the *Risorgimento*, traditions similar to those of American democracy.

The time will come when some great American artist or philosopher will win world-wide fame for a name like Bianchi or Bruni. At least this is not improbable. And when that day comes, the Whites and Browns of Italian origin will curse the stupidity, cowardice, or vanity that made their grandfathers prefer to write their names like the grocer at the street corner.

But until that day comes, how much of the discrimination which at one time beset part of the Italian element in the United States will remain? The answer—like all sincere and honest answers to psychological questions—cannot be direct and unqualified.

To begin with, this discrimination was urban, and what remains of it is still urban. City dwellers forget that some discrimination against new arrivals is a sort of natural law of city life; the incoming Irish felt it in the years before they took over Boston, Tammany Hall, and the police force. The Italians are also likely to forget that part of what happens to them here also happens in the north of Italy, where the working people, the poor white-collar class, and even the high school teachers are looked down upon by the professional people and the manufacturers. Many Italo-Americans are from the southern provinces. In Italy they would have felt the comic "superiority complex" which every stupid northerner betrays toward people of the south of his country.

But among the Italian farmers in the United States, the opposite is true. I have frequently eaten a joyous lunch outdoors in some leafy arbor with Italians who have succeeded in getting considerably more than a mere living out of the earth of Connecticut, Massachusetts, or California. No discrimination bothers them. They are exactly what they are, with the smiling philosophy and ageless wisdom of the Italian who lives on the soil. What discrimination there is works in the other direction. They have only ironical pity for American farmers who, according to them, can grow only one crop at a time and live on canned vegetables and six-month-old eggs while the wheat is coming in. And they save some of this pity for the rich estate owners round about who ask them to come and trim up their grounds at the wrong season, in a mistaken belief that the moon's influence over the proper cutting of trees and the bottling of wines is only the unscientific notion of an old Mediterranean people.

Saturday afternoons it is pathetic to see the children who work in the offices and factories of Boston, Hartford, and New Haven come back to the paternal farms. They are well dressed, possibly too well. They pull up in their little Fords, happy enough to see their parents—whom they love —and to take a glass of the golden Muscatel, which the Connecticut Italians are able to produce in a quality as heart-warming as that of the Muscatel of Sicily. Except at these gatherings, the Americanized children prefer a Martini or Manhattan. The parents are proud to have children who have "got there" and who talk such fluent English, peppered with "O.K." and "yeah." But at the same time they are also somewhat worried—not only because they know that however much they may think of going back to spend their old age in the Apennine village, especially dear now that they are so far away, their children are too American ever to go back. They are worried, too, about the fate of their children in America. An old farmer, who had come to the United States from Calabria and had vague plans of going back one day to live out his last years on his savings, said to me once,

My boys are happy here. If we go back to Italy we lose them. That's a law we have to accept. But will they be happy? This country is all for progress, no matter how hard you have to work for it. So are the people. But my boys are Italians. They are made for a calm, happy life. If there are more and longer depressions, our children will be worse off than the tramps are in Italy when there's a famine.

Such doubts (which, disturbingly enough, a careful reader also finds in Pearl Buck) annoy the children. The youngsters are already Americans; they want to be optimists at any cost. Life, however, is not something always to be viewed with optimism.

A word has to be added here about another form of discrimination. I mean the political type, which started to take form in 1940, when the nazi-fascist menace became evident to everyone. The Germans suddenly overran France (where too many of the governing class had too long sympathized with Hitler) ; then the Fascists dishonorably invaded the half-dead country. A majority of Italians at home disapproved this act of aggression, but for those who judge from the outside facts have the unfortunate faculty of counting for more than sterile intentions. Eighteen months later, in December, 1941, Mussolini's mad declaration of war against the United States rendered the situation even more bitter—at least among the Americans who have not yet realized that the war started in 1941 is a war of ideals, not of nationalities.

Liberal, democratic Italy had always urged upon Italo-Americans an absolute loyalty to their new country, coupled with the maintenance of cultural and spiritual bonds with the old. In this way free Italy contributed to the welfare of the United States by helping to form good American citizens. For you cannot make a good citizen out of a man who is intellectually and spiritually impoverished by being cut off from the only past he has had. If you do this to him, he becomes a savage, a bastard, or a robot.

Fascism had a different scheme. The ambassadors in Washington, the consuls in the big cities, Catholic and pseudo-Catholic propagandists, Fascists and pseudo-Fascists were all mobilized. Some very intelligent emissaries were even permitted to say, modestly, that they were not Fascists at all. Among these was one of my former secretaries who has written charming books in his time and who, at least when he thought of his poor father and of how the

latter would have died of shame, must often have suffered
for having fallen so low. But it is true that people can get
used quickly enough to moral abjection.

All these people tried to persuade Italo-Americans that
their prestige and their personal interests required them to
remain, in their hearts, exclusively Italian. They added,
of course, that a true Italian had to be a Fascist and that
any Italian who, being proud of his awareness of eight
centuries of Italian culture, remained faithful to the high,
pure traditions of the *Risorgimento* was a hypocrite and a
traitor.

The Italian-language newspapers of New York—such as
the *Progresso Italo-Americano*—with all the prestige imparted by a sixty-year existence, were easily influenced:
they repeated to their readers that their first duty was to
believe in and obey fascism, which, as they reiterated year
in and year out with increasing frenzy, would bring Italians a kind of glory they had never known in all their
tormented history. For the good people who in New York
read only the *Progresso* and the *Daily News,* and in the
other states other papers with scant international coverage,
it was easy to believe that the vain and empty conquest of
Ethiopia constituted a glory for all other peoples to be
jealous of and that the sanctions imposed on Italy by the
League of Nations were proof of the impotent hatred which
the democracies of England and France bore the irresistible force of fascist Italy. It goes without saying that they
hid from these poor readers, betrayed by the fascist
Italian-language sheets of New York, the fact that the sanctions were nothing but a farce staged by Neville Chamberlain and Laval as a favor to their friend Mussolini. Ac-

tually the sanctions were imposed only on imports which had nothing to do with carrying on a war, while nothing was done about the one sanction which would have been enough to kill fascism—shutting off the petroleum supply. The same papers instilled in Italo-American hearts the most dangerous of all possible feelings, the mania of persecution, out of which disloyalty and fifth-column tactics have grown in many countries. They told them that Italy was standing against the whole world and failed to tell them that the fascist regime, which they took to represent all Italy, had secret but most enthusiastic friends in all the Neville Chamberlains and Pierre Lavals. They even led these people to believe that the criminal nazi-fascist aggression in Spain was a beautiful and noble Christian crusade—and in this they had the aid of certain religious influences which will some day prove to have done the Catholic Church grave harm. Why should it seem strange that so many Italians who read in their favorite daily paper the same boastful lies, the same falsifications of history, ended by believing them? What people or national group could remain unaffected by the same lie passed out tirelessly, day after day, for years on end?

Yet American Italians frequently attempted to resist. Purely personal arguments sometimes threw the lies of the fascist propagandists out of tune. It was enough for some to recall that the great patriot and artist Toscanini, respected and loved everywhere in America, was horrified by fascism and that in Italy savage Italian bands had attacked and beaten him in typical fascist fashion, a thousand against one. In some places an infinitely smaller circumstance was enough: years ago echoes from my Rollins College lectures came to the ears of the thousands of Italians living in Tampa. They sent a deputation to Winter Park to deliver the following message: "We had been given to believe that the enemies of fascism hated Italy. But what you have said about Italy and its history and its nature has done more for the prestige of Italian people than all the tirades of the fascist agents. We thank you for it. We shall not forget."

In reality there was something which upset the Italians in America more than the fascist papers and the propagandists from Rome. This was the backing, sometimes unconscious, which important Americans, who were certainly not paid for doing so, gave the fascist cause. I say they were not paid. To be more exact, they were paid in decorations and flattering receptions and by a lot of friendly talk which fell from the lips of the pseudo-Roman mask of the Duce with well-rehearsed solemnity. Every time one of these Americans met an Italian—his barber or his doctor or his architect—he felt obliged to talk. It was like a religious mania. They had to tell, for the thousandth time, about their last trip to Italy. Actually it was also their first trip. Italian art and thought had never meant anything to them. They never went to Italy until they learned that a strikebreaker had become prime minister. Then they went like Arabs heading for Mecca.

That's a great man you have over there in Rome. We need a Mussolini here. Only a man like him can keep America from going to the dogs. He was very nice to me; we talked half an hour; he explained everything. He gave me his autographed photo. I have put it in a silver frame that cost $300. It will be a fine souvenir for my kids. Why, he's managed to get work out of Italians who . . .

At this point the barber, no less than the doctor or the architect, in spite of feeling flattered at being countrymen of such a genius, began to get a bit skeptical. They knew too well that the Italians are, and have always been, the most industrious workers in the world. But the great man went on: "How do you dare to doubt it? I have seen the cities on the Pontine marshes. They're jewels. If we could only do as well here. And five years ago those marshes were just useless land."

To all this the Italian listeners had no answer. Besides, if other Italians had worked miracles back home which reflected credit on the whole Italian nation—including the most recent immigrants who were unused to having credit reflected on them at all—so much the better. Why complain?

Besides, even if they had known that the drying of the Pontine marshes is one of the most astonishing cases of sterile graft in history, no one would have believed them. And if they had had documents to prove that the marshes used to represent a modest but sure national revenue from pasturage, whereas now, with the poor wheat crops and the artificial cities, the loss runs into millions, the worthy American gentlemen would have said to themselves, "I see. This fellow must be a dangerous radical, maybe a Communist."

One day in 1940 one of the most important manufacturers in the United States had the courage to explain to me the beauties of the Italian Corporative State—of which, naturally, he was superbly ignorant. I proved to him, calmly, by figures and by the testimony of Italian manufacturers whom he respected because they were as rich as he, that

Italian Corporatism has never functioned, that it is no more than a window dressing for foreigners and for Italians, a police system to stand guard over and enslave workers and owners alike. He replied: "Then how is it that all the Italians I talk to in New York as I have talked to you, say that more or less they agree with me?"

Since a group had formed around us in the room into which we had moved after our dinner, and since pompous smugness is the human frailty I like least, I explained to the old millionaire:

Because the brightest of these Italians think that it is useless to reply; that if you are naïve enough to take fascism for a way of saving society, it's better to leave you to your fate. As for the others, the ones who want to believe you, you may as well be told that you and the others who talk like you are guilty of treason (involuntary of course) against your country, for you are helping to form a fifth column by undermining the ideas which are the only bases for loyalty to America.

That is what happened in France and England. False conservatives of this type—the conservatives who make the revolutions of the future—admired Mussolini and Hitler during the years when the Chamberlains and the Lavals were leading their countries to the brink of the precipice.

Yet in 1940, when France was in danger of death, more than a hundred thousand Italians from Provence and Languedoc alone enlisted to form Italian divisions, setting up only two conditions: that they fight under an Italian flag and that they be sent against Germans rather than their own people. Whatever lists of these men were not lost in the catastrophe have been handed over by Vichy to the Fascists of the Armistice Commission. The men of Vichy are others who have been loud with resonant patriotic phrases.

In this world nothing exists alone. If you want loyalty to America, you must have loyalty among all Americans, especially those whose ancestors came—or so they think—in the Mayflower. When you find among the latter persons who put their personal interests above the supreme interests of the land, you will have no difficulty in finding fifth columnists among those who have come by way of Ellis Island.

But I had rather think about the hundred thousand Italians from Provence. The same loyalty to democracy which led them to offer up their lives for a free Europe can stir up the Italians in this country for the defense of a free America and a free world—and in great numbers. But this will only be if they are not discouraged and misled by being left at the mercy of ex-fascist leaders and preachers who may have changed their language, but not their spots.

CHAPTER XVII

Anti-Italian Legends: Italian Skepticism

ONE TRUE AND PERMANENT Italian trait strikes everyone who knows my compatriots, but it may strike in different ways: sympathizers call it "tolerance"; the others, "skepticism." The old Italian anti-clericals never hated the priests; at the most they made fun of them. This has been the style in Italian literature from Boccaccio down to the very Catholic Manzoni, with his Don Abbondio.

Something similar is true of the Italian Jews; we have never had real anti-Semitism; and the Fascists' anti-Semitic laws have been hated by all Italians. How could we have any anti-Semitism, with eighty thousand Jews lost in a nation of forty-four million individuals and since almost all these Jews are Sephardim, Spanish Jews often saturated with Occidental culture? In the rare cities where the Jewish element is somewhat more numerous, like Livorno and Pisa, one notices at most a slight tendency to repeat "Jewish stories," but not unkindly. The attitude is like that of the anti-clerical toward the priest to whom he will one day confide his children for their first communion. This is only the amiable tolerance of daily life, the fruit of a long history which has seen so much of it, although less than among the Chinese of yesterday, who, questioning each other, used to say: "What is your honorable religion? My own heap of ridiculous superstitions is . . ."

If skepticism there is, it has two aspects and two extremes, like everything else Italian. Among poor devils struggling for a niggardly living this alleged skepticism is especially a matter of mental laziness with respect to less immediate problems than that of hunger; their poor and humble philosophy is the *non te ne incarica* ("don't let it get you down") of the Neapolitan common folk. After all, the phenomenon is general. And if in Naples it is clearer sighted, the cause is —except in the case of harsh daily necessities—a psychological trait which is no less real because strangers have difficulty in recognizing it: people exaggerate their skepticism and opportunism because they are ashamed of them. Call this vanity or pride, if you like. But how many times, after one has succeeded in grasping this double meaning, the most cynical remarks betray rather the bitterness exemplified by the lines, certainly cynical in appearance, of a little-known poet of the fourteenth century, Bindo Bonichi:

> One way there is you may with people live:
> Avoid the thin and cultivate the fat,
> Listen and hark, to all approval give.

Especially among the most elevated minds, the skeptical remarks which one so frequently hears have often seemed to me only the bitter result of familiarity with life and history, a familiarity and a bitterness which it is not strange to find particularly profound in the intellectual elite of a nation whose history has seen so many painful trials. The complete disrespect of this elite for all official phraseology is only the counterpoise of the Italian bombast which prospers like a poisonous plant during periods of intellectual and spiritual decline—see, for instance, the pseudo-heroic jargon of the Fascists.

Among the Italians whom as a young man I most loved or

esteemed, a superficial observer would have detected a skepticism which, very often, was only the disguise of a lofty dignity. This same dignity explains the scarcity of memoirs by public personages in Italy in comparison with the number published in France and England. They have a sense of the mediocrity of what they have accomplished as opposed to what they had originally intended to do.

For thirty years Italy and the rest of Europe have pointed to Giolitti as the typical skeptic politician. Yet one day, when Giolitti was being attacked in the Chamber apropos of certain laws for provinces where the public life was not exactly exemplary, he turned to me and whispered, "They are right. Yes, just as right as if they were blaming a tailor for cutting a coat to fit a hunchback." But, on his feet, he replied in the subdued tones of an administrator, without the least sarcasm. He scorned those who made public exhibitions of their wit.

It was this same Giolitti who, at eighty-two, after his wife had died at their modest little estate at Cavour, went alone at two in the morning to kneel for hours beside her coffin in the little village church. I saw him some days later, and after a long silence he said simply: "Do you know what I found in my wife's prayerbook?—a letter I had written her from Rome thirty years ago during a cabinet crisis, in which I told her about the disgust I felt at having to live in the midst of the petty jealousies of politicians." Immediately thereafter he changed the subject of the conversation. This was the true Giolitti, but it is probable that future historians will be content with the handy legend that describes him as the archetype of skeptical Italian.

Personalities aside, the purest form of this skepticism may

be found in the most Italian novel that ever was, *The Betrothed*, by Manzoni. It is perhaps the very Italian character of *The Betrothed* which has kept foreign readers from finding in its pages all that we find there. When strangers heap their warmest praise on it—the first to do so being Goethe with his faithful Eckermann—the praise rings false in our ears, our own sentiment is so much more intense. Are the strangers in the wrong? Perhaps not; this may be but one more proof of the difficulty of feeling as an Italian feels. Manzoni is concerned only with souls, and he deliberately avoids knowing anything about political and religious systems. However gently expressed, his scorn for political incident, whether the war of Montferrat—"that beautiful war"—or the tumults at Milan under the Spaniards, appears on every page. On each page also are traits which, though far from obvious, give *The Betrothed* the privilege enjoyed by Shakespeare's *Tempest* of having a double appeal, such that after it has delighted us at sixteen we rediscover it with new emotion when we are forty. What one discovers in *The Betrothed* is above all the ironic pessimism of the Italian soul, too often mistaken for simple skepticism.

The legend of this skepticism has drawn wide attention, especially in the world of international politics, for a quality —or, others think, a defect—called the *combinazione*. I participated in not a few supreme councils of the post-war period and in other international conferences besides; all my colleagues did nothing—nor did I for that matter—but seek *combinazioni*. These colleagues included everyone from Lloyd George to Briand and from Curzon to Poincaré himself—I say "himself," because his too juridical mind hindered him from seeing the *combinazioni* he desired, down

deep, just as much as the others; he never succeeded in setting one in operation. These *combinazioni* are the very essence of normal political and social life. England's greatness in civil life became established only when this Italian
art became naturalized there and *combinazione* took the
name of "compromise." Why, then, should *combinazione*
draw criticism on Italians and still more so on the French
when they put aside their love for the letter of the law
and try it, while compromise is advanced as the supreme
proof of English wisdom? The answer is that the English
never talk of programs based on inviolable ideals. Consequently their *combinazioni* shock nobody.

In Italy, and still more so in France, we love to raise scaf-
foldings of general formulas; but since life is more demand-
ing than are formulas, we end by getting along with our adversaries. And that is well—only, so much noise has been
raised beforehand about the insurmountable conflict between the two programs.

Once, when I had negotiated a treaty of essential importance with our Slavic neighbors, the Nationalists came
to the Commission on Foreign Affairs to ask what had been
my guiding idea. And I, slightly boastful—for in truth I
had tried above all to serve my country—replied with a
quip in which there was, as it happened, a bit of truth: "I
wanted to divide the dissatisfaction equitably between the
two countries." The reply was so thoroughly Italian that for
an instant—a very short instant—it did not displease even
my adversaries.

CHAPTER XVIII

Anti-Italian Realities: Fascism

FASCISM IS TOTALITARIANISM and can be nothing else. It is eclectic enough to embrace all things save one— free discussion. Discussion would kill it instantly. But is totalitarianism not the state of mind most foreign to the Italian character? The very essence of this character is an individualism which renders incomprehensible to Italians the *zusammenmarchieren* of the Germans. Of all peoples the Italians are perhaps the most particularist; history has made them so. Like the Belgian, the Italian has been conscious that his liberty and dignity have developed in the free cities. The Fascists knew what they were about when they broke off the free administration of the cities and imposed on them a *Podestà* named by the Minister of the Interior. In doing so they simply gave one more proof that the patriotism of tyrannical regimes consists of phrases, not of acts. They worked for the destruction of historic bonds which have sustained the Italians throughout centuries of glory and misfortune.

In my travels about the United States I have often met those picturesque types, the old Italian anarchists. Some of them are dangerous; more are only amiably insane; but all of them—speaking of course, of the sincere ones—bear a certain nobility about them. The old patriotism, they said, was a hindrance to the attainment of their wider conception of liberty. In Chicago I met an old anarchist from Lunigiana,

and when I began to give him, in the patois of his youth, news
of his native town, Sarzane, and of its rival, Spezia, the eyes
of the childish rebel filled with tears.

The ancient bond between Italian generations is the city,
which carries us back to pre-Roman times. Even under pre-
Caesarian Rome, Italy was only a federation of cities, each
free to live its own interior life and to control the land
around it. It was only with the long series of Caesars, set on
the throne by the Praetorians, that what would today be
called the totalitarian state was imposed upon Italy. At that
time the totalitarian state ruined Italy, as the Fascists also
have done. As a consequence of the destruction of local vitality which the imperial regime of Rome necessitated, the
German tribes, moving toward the south, succeeded for a
time in establishing themselves on the peninsula.

The peculiar genius of Italy is particularist; the opposite
of particularism is fascism, which is totalitarian by necessity. The history of Italy proves that the true social order
under which its people progress and prosper has nothing in
common with the suffocating uniformity of the Fascists. The
Middle Ages, which were the time of faction and civil war
and antagonism between the common people and the great,
were also the era of our greatest poets, painters, sculptors,
and architects, as also of the Genoese and Florentine banks,
of Venetian fleets, and of Lombard commerce. This was a
nonimperialistic Italy, which happened to possess the empire of the Mediterranean.

After the 1918 armistice those poor white-collar prole-
tarian failures who furnished fascism with its most naïve
and sincere members could not understand the greatness of
the Italian Middle Ages, in which everything was disorder

and life, as they could not understand, and consequently repudiated, the human magnanimity of the men of the *Risorgimento*, from Mazzini to Cavour.

Strangers who want to find out what Italy truly is, beneath the aspect which has been imposed upon it by fascism,
should meditate upon her history—a history so long and
with such marked alternations of fortune that episodes several years in length disappear from the perspective. Moreover, everyone should say to himself, in Italy and outside,
that it is futile to proclaim the failure of democracy, since
democracy is always an ideal to be attained and not a fact
behind us. In Italy, for example, it was only on the eve of
the World War that universal suffrage was adopted—a real
though bloodless revolution accomplished without the least
disorder. Two years later Italy, under universal suffrage,
accepted war against the Central Powers, although in the
same way as it would have accepted the inevitability of an
earthquake, for the country had not yet been attacked. Only
after a severe reverse and an invasion did the Italians begin
to feel the war as a national duty; it was no longer a matter
of provinces to be conquered, but of standing and dying in
order to retain mastery of the homeland. The sudden Italian
unity in the teeth of a disaster which the Austrians expected
to be their downfall was one of the finest moral spectacles
of the whole European war; but, the easily accepted legend
notwithstanding, everything took place in Italian hearts;
there was no exterior manifestation.

When peace returned, with six hundred thousand Italian
dead scattered on the Carso and the Alps, in Champagne and
in Macedonia, soapbox statesmen tried to take away our
pride of victory by telling the Italian people that since it

had not taken Dalmatia, it had been beaten. In spite of that, and in spite of economic obstacles, the Italian people went back to work. Our alleged excesses of the post-war years were no worse than those in France and England, where, as I have already said, there were more strikes than in Italy.

But what happened in Italy was this: a faction which got power in its hands by violence and fraud set about excusing its violence and fraud by defaming, with the cleverest publicity possible, the people which it had enslaved. They let it be believed that the Italians, the most laborious of peoples, were undisciplined sluggards whom it was necessary to "correct" with castor oil and to "elevate" with pseudo-Roman rhetoric. All the intellectually indolent of Europe ended by believing this, for the Fascists were the discoverers of the axiom which Nazism later applied in Germany and Stalin, for internal purposes only, used in Russia: "a lie often enough repeated becomes the truth."

But not only is the Italian nation nourished on ageless tradition, it also goes through periods of extreme ill health without losing its equally ageless ability to renew itself. It was thus after the long night of the year 1000. And it was thus after the doleful Spanish period of the seventeenth and eighteenth centuries. The day will come when we shall see that neither slavery nor the sterile adventures of invasion in Spain and of war against France, England, and the United States could succeed in making us lose our love of liberty and our—perhaps unbounded—individualism.

CHAPTER XIX

The Italians and the Future of Europe

THE TRAGIC POET Alfieri wrote at the beginning of the nineteenth century that nowhere in the world does the human plant flourish as it does in Italy. The more one gets to know Alfieri, both as man and as tragic poet, the more one has the impression that when he wrote this he was thinking especially of himself.

Young Alfieri was perishing of boredom in the lugubrious Turin of the second half of the eighteenth century. He was rich enough to undertake the then classic Grand Tour. Returning to Italy, he scandalized his peers by his admiration for the English who had decapitated Charles I. He wanted reform. But what could he do in the Italy of that time, an Italy of *abbés* and academies, of sonnets for girls who took husbands and for girls who took the veil? In twenty years of obstinate labor, driven by his desire to awaken Italians to their *virtu prisca*, he gave his country a dramatic repertory which succeeded in creating a whole generation of "tyrant-haters." Parini struck off the phrase *odiator dei tiranni* to fit Alfieri himself. Alfieri's *Life*, the most humane of his writings, shows what superhuman effort he made.

The truth of Alfieri's remark about the human plant is that nowhere in the world are contrasts deeper than among Italians. In Italy men are like the country—very few agreeable and charming hills, but either plains (and sometimes swamps) or else sharp, proud mountains. There is no middle ground.

This is just the opposite of the impression which Montaigne got from his travels in Italy:

"They have commonly more faire women, and fewer foule than we; but in rare and excellent beauties I thinke we match them. The like I judge of their wits; of the vulgar sort they have evidently many more. Blockishness is without all comparison more rare amongst them: but for singular wits, and of the highest pitch, we are no whit behind them." [1]

Montaigne's impression is correct—but correct with reference to the Italian society that he knew—still blossoming in the rays of the Renaissance which had created a new social type, the accomplished man-of-society. This type—such as Castiglione described him in the *Perfect Courtesan*—was exceptional, but not entirely unknown, as it was also in the France of Louis XIV. The development of courts had brought it to Italy a century earlier. Montaigne had seen talent only in the service of a few tyrants: secretaries, functionaries, house pets, poets, people in general who learned rapidly to know and to exploit all the resources of their minds, to impress their worth upon their overlord so as to share longer a small part of his power. Refined though they were, they could not help being the "wits of the vulgar sort" which Montaigne considered them.

But Machiavelli, an Italian who was in contact with a whole world which of necessity escaped Montaigne, found that Italians were "peerless in individual action," but mediocre when acting in groups. Even at that time, indeed, the supreme characteristic of individualism—the ease with which they could emigrate—was not lacking. The via dei

[1] *The Essayes of Montaigne,* translated by John Florio, 1632, New York, the Modern Library, p. 797.

Lucchesi in Rome and Lombard Street in London date from the sixteenth century. And so does the tragic tradition, so thoroughly Italian, of accepting exile rather than change faith, an exile which embitters those with disappointed ambitions, but purifies those who suffer for the sake of conscience. Already in the fifteenth century Pontano was writing: "In our populous cities we see throngs of people who have voluntarily left their homes behind. Qualities and virtues one can bring with one."

Even artists, although their sensations necessarily remained bound up with their native Florence or Siena, thought it a duty to express their universalism. "Only he who has learned everything," Ghiberti boasted, "is not a foreigner anywhere; even without fortune or friends, he is a citizen of every city."

The marvelous expansion of national sentiment between 1815 and 1860 led Italian writers to exaggerate the moral laxity which the earlier period may have left behind it. Especially since it was formulated in view of a patriotic goal, nineteenth-century criticism in Italy had become a sort of facile, puritanical generalizing, the product of upright but somewhat narrow minds. Yet at least these later Italians owed much to the past of which they were too ashamed. As if the politics of the France of Commynes had been any more scrupulous than those of the Italy of Machiavelli! Before Machiavelli, Commynes wrote political precepts which would have been similar to those of the *Prince* except for one thing—the genius was lacking. These Italians owed the past the fact that they had escaped the "esprit de galanterie" which in France nearly killed love, and that desire to shine which provided France with so many valiant, honorary generals whose names are no longer remembered. During the century of saccharine arcadias the Italians could become impassioned over a sonnet contest, but at least they remained indifferent to the taste for ribbons with which the masters of the Louvre and of the Tuileries have so often tried to keep a grip on the French.

And if, during the reawakening of nationalities, the two peoples which the nineteenth century found disunited, the Germans and the Italians, expressed their ideal so differently, this is to be explained in terms of our past. From the start the Italians set up the limits of their national aspirations at the Alps and Quarnero, and they always linked their aspiration—the humane Mazzini as much as the bookish Gioberti—with a corresponding project of European harmony which was to complement the national resurgence. The Germans, on the other hand, embraced with confused exaltation all the lands which some Alaric, some Barbarossa or other, had trampled down, viewing the Slavs of Prague only as intruders, talking of Verona as the appanage of the fabulous Dietrich, and thinking of Trieste as a port stolen from the Holy Empire.

Certainly the discreet dignity of Italian intellectual life, as it appeared at the end of the nineteenth century after decades of independence, was too complex and delicate for eyes rendered daily more myopic by the easy mysteries of the cinema. Yet it will be among those Italians who talked simply of "country" and rarely, as if with repugnance, of "fatherland," that we shall some day see the most perfect fruition of Italian variety and individualism and nonconformity. They were the living antithesis of the threat of uniformity which has been suspended over the agrarian masses by fascism, nationalist and racist propaganda, and, in America, by the monotony of Main Street, where to be different is to be indecent.

While the English gentleman is the fruit of a long social and moral tradition, these Italians were the intellectual end-products of our history plus the spiritual preoccupations of the *Risorgimento* which worked as a sort of Reformation in the aristocracy and the middle class. These Italians have never died out even under the sometimes bloody, sometimes theatrical constraints of fascism. Like members of a prohibited religion, they recognize each other by a mere word.

The masses of artisan and peasant Italy are still among the spiritual marvels of Europe. In 1917 and 1918, during the long months of the invasion of Friuli and other parts of Venetia, not a single peasant consented to furnish information to the enemy. The documents of the Austro-Hungarian Grand General Staff point to this fact as one of the proofs of the difficulties encountered by the Austro-German Intelligence. Only those familiar with the occasional humiliating failures caused by the peasants on so many fronts—especially in Flanders—can feel what this fact signifies.

Returning from a war which had cost six hundred thousand lives, the Italian people asserted itself in the political arena in 1919, with a desire for a new deal and for sincerity whose excesses and disturbances should not have misled people regarding their strength and value. I spent many days of my life in the Parliament elected in 1919. I remember its weaknesses and its stains—for example the grotesque Misiano, who boasted that he had deserted from the army, and a few other "reds," almost all of whom later became partisans of Mussolini. All in all it was an assembly representative of a people who aspired only to reasonable social reforms. It would have been easily satisfied with a bit of the breadth of mind which the English conservatives displayed in a similar situation in the first decades of the nineteenth century.

Some of the Italian "upper classes" preferred the easier but more dangerous game of suppression by force. This has happened so often in history that, for my part, I catalogue certain "conservatives" as among the most efficacious artificers of future revolutions. What had never before been seen was the gigantic propaganda organization which in order to excuse the use of violence has for years defamed my people, letting it be understood that the Italians were anarchist do-nothings whom it was necessary to "correct" and to "elevate." To assure the glory of its own future, fascism and its tory supporters did not hesitate to attempt to heap dishonor on the Italian people.

At the end of this book a question arises: what will be the Italian role in the Europe of the future? History has already shown us the two opposite ways of coördinating different European nationalities. One was the way of imperial Austria, and, after 1867, imperial and royal Austria-Hungary. We ourselves saw it at work, this great power composed of ten different nationalities whose only link was the family interest of the Hapsburgs, with their eternal maxim "Divide and rule." The inevitable result was the ultimatum to Serbia —and the war of 1914–18. The other example of a historical formation which bridged over nationalities is Switzerland, where the three—Germans, French, and Italians—live, as I have shown in a previous chapter, on terms of equality despite the numerical disproportion between them. Each Swiss is conscious of his pride and love for his German, French, or Italian culture, but a rational desire for mutual understanding and a common love of liberty make him ally it with a superior patriotism toward the Helvetic Union. And this is the result of anything but a special dispensation. The entire first half of the nineteenth century was filled with bickering between the cantons.

The same was true in America in the first years of the Union, where solidarity was also the reward for laborious effort. Hamilton himself wrote: "The concurrence of thirteen distinct sovereign wills is requisite, under the Confederation, to the complete execution of every important measure that proceeds from the Union. It has happened as was to be foretold: the measures of the Union have not been executed. . . ." And in a still more suggestive passage, for it could have been applied, more than a century later to the European politics of 1936 regarding sanctions called for by the Article 16 of the Covenant at the moment of the invasion of Ethiopia:

"The rulers of the respective members, whether they have a constitutional right to do it or not, will undertake to judge the propriety of the measures themselves. They will consider the conformity of the thing proposed or required to their immediate interests or aims. . . . If, therefore, the measures of the Confederacy cannot be executed without the intervention of the particular administrations, there will be little prospect of their being executed at all." [2]

In spite of the bond of sentiment created by a war waged in common against England, in spite of the identity of language—a factor whose importance is perhaps often exaggerated—Hamilton went through painful doubt about the

[2] *The Federalist*, Number XV.

cohesion of his country in the first decades of American independence.

Our old mutual antipathies, our wars and the accompanying noise of racist and nationalist propaganda, prevent our realizing that the feeling that we are Europeans is stronger than we admit. This is not due to any merit of ours, but is because today Europe herself produces new national units, which rise about her a thousand times more different from Europe than any of the European nationalities are different from each other.

Asia has always been a very different world from the tiny Europe which juts out from it. By occidentalizing Asia we have brought it nearer, but the proximity is only material and makes us the more conscious of the profound differences of spiritual and social structure which separate it from us.

North America in its turn aids the formation of a European sentiment by the fact that the American personality has developed in a way so detached from ours, especially in the last two generations. Let the Europeans who are the most skeptical about the future of Europe remember their instinctive sensations on their return home after a long stay in the United States. Whether they have been annoyed by certain aspects of the excessive standardization of American life or whether—like me—they have enjoyed the warmth and spontaneity which one so often feels in the United States, even among the most cultivated, they cannot fail to notice how much more they feel at home as soon as they arrive in one of our great ports, small difference whether Cherbourg or Genoa, Liverpool or Rotterdam.

It is no dream. Throughout the Middle Ages the Italian communes did nothing but skirmish with each other; even the genius of Dante did not succeed in detaching itself from the municipal strife of his time. His apostrophes against Siena and Pisa are heavier with hatred than the *Gott strafe England* of 1914 and 1940. The fact is that when one hates a neighbor one knows well and whose language one speaks, the hatred has more savor.

After all, the concept of the absolute sovereignty of the state was born of monarchical absolutism—tempered at first by what remained of feudalism and later by the liberal currents of the nineteenth century. It has developed again—made more dangerous by the patriotic intoxication of the democracies and a thousand times worse yet by the pagan deification of the nation preached by the Nazis and Fascists. But the nationalisms and their violences will one day follow the curve of religious hatreds. In the time when joyful, savage violence was being done the Protestant minorities in France and Italy and later to the Catholic minority in England, it seemed that these things, too, would have no end. The horror of the war unleashed by Hitler in 1939 and by the whole Axis in 1940 and 1941 will hasten the outcome.

The *realpolitikers* forget that through long periods of history slavery was a natural necessity. Yet not only has slavery been suppressed, but also more has been done toward its suppression in the half century following the war of 1861 in America than during the ten preceding centuries.

Those who were young in Europe between 1900 and 1914 have seen one great social transformation with their own eyes—the disappearance of the duel. When I tell my children that as a young man in 1905 I fought a duel, they listen in delighted amusement, as if I were telling detective stories.

There is thus no rational difficulty in admitting that war

as a juridical institution may disappear. But is this saying that the great historical revolution is now in sight? I should not dare affirm it for all countries; at least not for the Germans—or the Prussians, to be more lenient—as long as they have not learned that wars are not always fought away from home. But certainly the Italians have learned it. And the criminal sterility of the war that fascism imposed on them in 1940 against Great Britain and in 1941 against the United States has finally persuaded even the puny but vociferous Italian minority described in this book. Events have taught the lesson love could not teach.

In Europe and in America those who will not understand are the groups that from 1919 to 1939 continued to consider criminal the surrender of the least parcel of our national sovereignty in favor of organisms more vast and more complex than our contemporary states; this was clear in 1940, when in France even the men who were most decided not to betray the British alliance stood bewildered—bewildered rather than hesitant—when Churchill with his impetuous genius proposed a complete fusion of the two colonial empires, with parity of direction and prestige.

That the growing need of international understanding and harmony should not have been grasped by the fascist and nazi chiefs is not only natural, it is also an additional argument for the inevitability of a movement toward a European entente. When the Italian people has recovered its liberty, its disgust will be only the more profound for the insane preaching of international hatred inflicted on it by the Fascists. Mussolini showed at certain rare moments that he recognized this state of mind in the Italian people by alternating occasional threats of "explosion" with affirmations in favor of peace such as his declaration which President Nicholas Murray Butler reports in his account of a conversation he had in March, 1934, with the Italian Dictator: "There must be no more wars; another war would not only ruin Italy, but it would also destroy civilization." [3] Only, at that same moment Mussolini was preparing the war in Ethiopia, whence issued, as inevitable results, first the invasion of Spain, and later the destruction of Czechoslovakia, the invasion of France, and the war of the Axis against the United States.

Once all peoples have seen its incalculable effects—like the elimination of war—the organization of Europe will progress relatively faster than did other transformations such as that of religious tolerance after the centuries of religious wars. Nothing—especially after the criminal wars of 1939 and 1940—can longer stop the growing spiritual forces which are on the march. These spiritual forces will show the world of what a renaissance the Italians will be capable once they have emerged from the abject moral lethargy of fascism—and probably not of spiritual energy alone. Peoples are controlled both by ideals and by self-interest. Not all Italians are quite clear in their own minds that they are happier in an international atmosphere than in a country closed off by hermetically-sealed frontiers. No other nation in Europe can furnish anything like their list of men who have made themselves famous in international enterprises, from the Florentines and the Lombards who ruled the commerce and the banking of all fourteenth and fifteenth-century Europe down to the Mazarins, the Alberonis, the Bonapartes and Disraelis who—having left Italy —directed or created Empires. They had faults and ambi-

[3] Nicholas Murray Butler, *Across the Busy Years*, New York, Scribner's, 1939, II, 165.

tions, but they never lacked an international instinct even in the midst of their worst and most cruel follies, not excluding the follies of Napoleon. If to these famous names I dared add certain relatively humble groups, I could bear witness that while the most powerful collective service of the Far East in the nineteenth and the first decade of the twentieth centuries—the administration of the Chinese Imperial Customs—had a chief of genius in the Irish Sir Robert Hart, his most esteemed collaborators, those whose ideal was teamwork, were the Italians. My long stay in China permits me to testify. At Geneva, in the brief Golden Age of the League of Nations—before a few functionaries of my country were corrupted or terrified by fascism—the Italian bureau heads were among the best and certainly among the most devoted to the ideal of the Covenant.

The intellectual immaturity of the Fascists made them think—when, rarely, they were trying to think—that there would be advantages in an Italian autarchy, sufficient to itself and threatening others with clamorous if ungenuine preparations for war. Let a more-or-less federated Europe have only a few years, under whatever exterior aspect, and there will no longer be one Italian, even among the rare ones who were Fascists with clear conscience, who will not admit that his people, his interests, and his ideas are much more at ease in the new situation.

What is the real source of Europe's suffering? What was the source even before the frightful first day of September, 1939, when Hitler plunged into the conquest of Poland? This source especially: that Europe had become too cramped for its economic and intellectual resources. Before 1914 one could still, if necessary, be simply French or English, or

Italian. Today it is no longer possible. Did not Mussolini, who for years proclaimed that fascism is not an article for foreign consumption, try with all his strength, a few years before the war of 1939, to transplant fascism into Spain, Yugoslavia, Hungary, France, and even Switzerland?

The war of 1939 will have shown the blindest that nothing is more unreasonable and dangerous than the exclusive substitution of the abstract idea of the nation for the reality of social life. Certainly Italy was the first, with Mazzini and Cavour, to make powerful use of the principle of nationality to combat the domination of the empire of the Hapsburgs.

But it is an invariable rule that when a principle or an idea has rendered enormous service to one generation, entirely changed situations emerge. If the idea which provoked the transformation develops by itself, its life can be prolonged. But often the idea stops developing and reclines on its glorious past; the new generation bows before the tabernacle up to the time when the idea's consequences begin to look dangerous. Thus it is that the bloody violence of the Nazis and the Fascists has almost made us forget—so much do we fear any sort of national intoxication—that the Italian apostles of the idea of nationality never considered nations to be ends in themselves. In his half-century of struggle for the liberty and unity of Italy, Mazzini never ceased to affirm that the triumph of nationalities should finally be crowned by a European union.

This is the reality of the future. The crimes and sufferings of the war which Nazis and Fascists forced on Europe in 1939 and on the United States in December, 1941, will only hasten its arrival. The long history of the Italians will permit them to be ready for the broader framework which this future will create for the peoples of Europe. They will thus prove how faithful they have remained to their true past and to what extent they have remained Italian in the profound meaning of the word as it was understood by our highest minds from Dante to Mazzini.

Recent Books on Italian Problems

THE VERY NATURE of this book having obliged me to insist on the ephemeral character of fascism, some readers may wish to know where they may find more detailed information.

Origins of Fascism

Borgese, G. A. Goliath, the March of Fascism. New York, Viking, 1937.

Keene, F. Neither Liberty nor Bread. New York, Harper, 1940.

Lussu, E. Road to Exile. New York, Covici, Friede, 1936.

Salvemini, G. The Fascist Dictatorship in Italy. New York, Holt, 1927; London, Cape.

Sforza, C. Makers of Modern Europe. New York, Bobbs Merrill, 1930; London, Elkin and Marrott.

—— European Dictatorships. New York, Coward-McCann, 1931; London, Allen and Unwin.

Sturzo, L. Italy and Fascism. New York, Harcourt, 1927; London, Faber.

Diplomatic and Economic Developments of Fascism

Binchy, D. Church and State in Fascist Italy. London, Oxford University Press, 1941.

Salvemini, G. Under the Axe of Fascism. New York, Viking, 1936.

—— Mussolini diplomate. Paris, Grasset.

Sforza, C. Europe and Europeans. New York, Bobbs Merrill, 1936; London, Hatrop.

—— Fifty Years of War and Diplomacy in the Balkans. New York, Columbia Univ. Press, 1940.

Trentin, S. La Crise du droit et de l'État. Paris-Brussels, Eglantine, 1935.

Collections of the following periodicals: *La Libertà* (Paris); *Giustizia e libertà* (Paris); *Giovine Italia* (Paris).

Psychology and Moral History of the Italian People

Croce, B. History of Italy, 1871–1915, tr. by Cecilia M. Ady. New York, Oxford University Press, 1929.

Bosis, L. de. Story of My Death. New York, Oxford University Press, 1933.

Lussu, E. Sardinian Brigade. New York, Knopf, 1939.

Pentad. The Remaking of Italy. London, Penguin.

Silone, I. Fontamara. New York, Smith, 1934.

—— Bread and Wine. New York, Harper, 1937.

Salvatorelli, L. Concise History of Italy. New York, Oxford University Press, 1940.

Sturzo, L. Church and State. New York, Longmans, 1939.